People in the News (Lucent Books) (Library Binding)

Tina Fey: Queen of Comedy $31.52

Tina Fey, one of the most prominent is well known for her work on shows Night Live and 30 Rock. As a writer a changed the way people see female com

#2002156   M. Shofner   Available

Grade:789   Dewey:791

Cristiano Ronaldo $31.52

This contemporary biography series profiles the lives of some of today's most prominent newsmakers; whether covering contributions and achievements or notorious deeds, books in this series examine why ...

#1919092   G. Stewart   Available:08/07/2015   128 pgs

Grade:789   Dewey:796.33

Prince William and Duchess Kate $31.52

A biography of William and Kate, the Duke and Duchess of Cambridge

#1919146   J. MacKay   Available:08/07/2015   128 pgs

Grade:789   Dewey:941.08

Robert Kirkman $31.52

#1919143   A. Woog   Available:04/21/2015   128 pgs

Grade:789   Dewey:B

Jennifer Lawrence $31.52

#1919142   G. Stewart   Available:03/26/2015   128 pgs

Grade:789   Dewey:791.43

Taylor Swift
Superstar Singer

By Katie Kawa

Portions of this book originally appeared in
Taylor Swift by Cherese Cartlidge

LUCENT PRESS

Published in 2017 by
Lucent Press, an Imprint of Greenhaven Publishing LLC
353 3rd Avenue
Suite 255
New York, NY 10010

Designer: Deanna Paternostro
Editor: Katie Kawa

Cataloging-in-Publication Data

Names: Kawa, Katie.
Title: Taylor Swift: superstar singer / Katie Kawa.
Description: New York : Lucent Press, 2017. | Series: People in the news |
Includes index.
Identifiers: ISBN 9781534560253 (library bound) | ISBN 9781534560260
(ebook)
Subjects: LCSH: Swift, Taylor, 1989---Juvenile literature.Country musi-
cians--United States--Biography--Juvenile literature.Singers--United
States--Biography--Juvenile literature.
Classification: LCC ML3930.S989 K39 2017 | DDC 782.421642092--dc23

Printed in the United States of America

CPSIA compliance information: Batch #CW17KL: For further information contact Greenhaven Publishing LLC,
New York, New York at 1-844-317-7404.

Please visit our website, www.greenhavenpublishing.com. For a free
color catalog of all our high-quality books, call toll free 1-844-317-7404
or fax 1-844-317-7405.

Contents

Foreword

We live in a world where the latest news is always available and where it seems we have unlimited access to the lives of the people in the news. Entire television networks are devoted to news about politics, sports, and entertainment. Social media has allowed people to have an unprecedented level of interaction with celebrities. We have more information at our fingertips than ever before. However, how much do we really know about the people we see on television news programs, social media feeds, and magazine covers?

Despite the constant stream of news, the full stories behind the lives of some of the world's most newsworthy men and women are often unknown. Who was Taylor Swift before she was a pop music phenomenon? What does LeBron James do when he is not playing basketball? What inspired Elon Musk to dream as big as he does?

This series aims to answer questions such as these about some of the biggest names in pop culture, sports, politics, and technology. While the subjects of this series come from all walks of life and areas of expertise, they share a common magnetism that has made them all captivating figures in the public eye. They have shaped the world in some unique way, and—in many cases—they are poised to continue to shape the world for many years to come.

These biographies are not just a collection of basic facts. They tell compelling stories that show how each figure grew to become a powerful public personality. Each book aims to paint a complete, realistic picture of its subject—from the challenges they overcame to the controversies they caused. In doing so, each book reinforces the idea that even the most famous faces on the news are real people who are much more complex than we are often shown in brief video clips or sound bites. Readers are also reminded that there is even more to a person than what they present to the world through social media posts, press releases, and interviews. The whole story of a person's life can only be discovered by digging beneath the surface of their public persona, and that is what this series allows readers to do.

The books in this series are filled with enlightening quotes from speeches and interviews given by the subjects, as well as quotes and anecdotes from those who know their story best: family, friends, coaches, and colleagues. All quotes are noted to provide guidance for further research. Detailed lists of additional resources are also included, as are timelines, indexes, and unique photographs. These text features come together to enhance the reading experience and encourage readers to dive deeper into the stories of these influential men and women.

Fame can be fleeting, but the subjects featured in this series have real staying power. They have fundamentally impacted their respective fields and have achieved great success through hard work and true talent. They are men and women defined by their accomplishments, and they are often seen as role models for the next generation. They have left their mark on the world in a major way, and their stories are meant to inspire readers to leave their mark, too.

Introduction

Making It Personal

Taylor Swift rose to country music stardom when she was a teenager, thanks to her ability to write songs that are deeply personal and powerfully relatable. She then used that same talent to make the jump from country music to pop music, reaching new heights of fame and success. She is now a global superstar, but her popularity remains rooted in the same personal approach to songwriting that first drew fans to her music more than a decade ago.

Swift has achieved unprecedented success by speaking to young fans through her music. Although her music has a broad appeal, she is best known as a voice for young women. Her songs speak to the changes many girls and women go through as they grow up—from first heartbreaks to moving to a new city. In writing about her own life experiences, Swift has forged a strong connection with her passionate fans.

Swift has been known for her personal lyrics ever since she first appeared on the country music scene. When she was just 19 years old, a writer for the *New York Times* stated that she was "more in touch with her inner life than most adults."[1] Swift's gift for turning introspection into hit songs has fueled her career. In a 2013 interview with *Entertainment Weekly*, she said, "My experience with songwriting is usually so confessional, it's so drawn

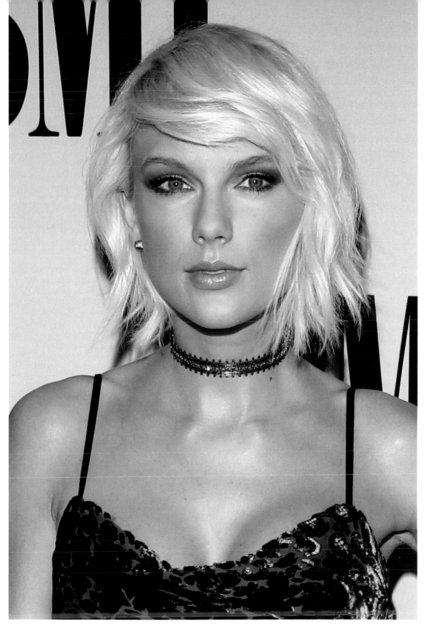

Taylor Swift became famous for writing about her life experiences. Her songs come from a personal place that her fans can relate to.

from my own life and my own stories."[2] Her ability to create songs that reflect the universal experiences of growing up has given young women—who often feel like they are without a voice—a catalog of songs that seem to speak directly to them.

Swift's ability to form connections with her fans has only grown as she has branched out into the worlds of acting, advertising, and activism. The teenager who showed up in Nashville, Tennessee, with a guitar and songs she wrote herself has become a woman with incredible influence on music, fashion, and popular culture.

Social Media Superstar

How did Taylor Swift become a global pop culture phenomenon? Her songwriting talent is a big part of her success. However, it is not the only part. Her ability to use social media to her advantage has been a key to her superstar status. Scott Borchetta, the founder of Big Machine Records who first signed Swift to a record deal, described her as "remarkably and extraordinarily media savvy."[3] Swift knows how to adapt to changes in social media in order to stay in touch with her fans. Her social media presence has evolved from her early days of using the social networking website MySpace to share her music with fans. Today, she maintains a strong presence on social media platforms that include Twitter, Instagram, and Tumblr.

The way Swift uses social media is different from the way some other celebrities use it. As *Los Angeles Times* writer Randy Lewis stated, "She has brilliantly created a level of conversation with her followers that most other entertainers can only dream of."[4] Swift uses her social media accounts to interact with her fans, using those accounts not just as promotional tools but as a way to create what Lewis called an "ongoing dialogue"[5] with her fans. That dialogue makes her fans feel as if they have a closer connection with her than fans have with other artists, which only reinforces the message Swift sends out in her relatable songs.

Swift carefully manages her social media presence, which has made her the target of critics. They describe the photos she shares

Swift's relationship with her fans is an important part of her public image and a major factor in her success.

as looking "fake" and "forced."[6] However, criticism of her public image has not stopped Swift from sharing parts of her life with fans and inspiring them to do the same with her.

Creating a Connection

Swift's career has been built on the connection she has made and maintained with her fans, especially her young female fans. Although she has faced challenges that range from childhood bullies to current critics of her public image, Swift has used those challenges to enrich her music and encourage her fans. As Lewis stated, "She has a vision of how to use her fame constructively."[7] Swift has become a role model for her millions of fans, and that is something she does not take lightly. In a 2009 interview with MSNBC, she said, "Every single time I look down in the audience and I see somebody singing the words back to me, it makes it all worth it."[8] The strong bond between Swift and her fans has impacted both the people singing those words in the audience and the woman who wrote them.

Chapter **One**

Pennsylvania Roots

Taylor Swift named her record-breaking 2014 album *1989* to celebrate the year she was born. On December 13, 1989, Andrea Swift gave birth to a daughter and named her Taylor Alison. Taylor's mother deliberately gave her daughter a first name that would work for either a boy or a girl. Andrea was a marketing executive and a practical woman. She and her husband Scott, who worked as a stockbroker, were both successful businesspeople who wanted their daughter to have every advantage in the professional world. Andrea thought it would be beneficial for their daughter to have a name that could belong to a man or woman, so others would not limit her opportunities based on her gender as soon as they read her name.

Andrea and Scott raised their daughter in Wyomissing, Pennsylvania, which is a suburb of Reading and about 64 miles (103 km) northwest of Philadelphia. Taylor was born into a loving family whose support has been a source of strength for her as her star continues to rise.

An Ideal Childhood

Growing up, Taylor always thought of her date of birth as being special for two reasons. Although she was born on the 13th, which many people regard as an unlucky number, Taylor turned the old superstition around. She considers the number 13 to be her lucky number. In a 2009 interview with MTV, she said, "Basically whenever a 13 comes up in my life, it's a good thing."[9] Taylor has also said she loves that she was born so close to a major holiday, and she enjoys having Christmas-themed birthday parties.

When Taylor was two years old, the Swift family welcomed a new baby—Taylor's younger brother, Austin. After Austin's birth, Andrea quit her job to stay home and be a full-time mother to her two children. Taylor and Austin lived in a house where they were encouraged and loved by both of their attentive parents.

The Swift family was financially well off. Wyomissing is a wealthy suburb, and the family owned and lived on a Christmas tree farm when Taylor was young. The family also took frequent vacations to the beach in Stone Harbor, New Jersey. There, the Swifts enjoyed spending time together in the water and on their boat. When speaking about her childhood in 2008, Taylor called it "the most amazing, magical way to grow up."[10]

Taylor has always had a warm and loving relationship with her family. Because she and Austin are close in age, they spent a lot of time together playing games, watching cartoons, and goofing around. Taylor also believes she is lucky to have a mother and father who are both involved in their children's lives. She refers to her father as "a big teddy bear,"[11] and she has always had an especially close relationship with her mother. Taylor spent many happy hours as a child baking, shopping, going horseback riding, and taking long walks around the farm with Andrea. In an interview with the *Washington Post*, Taylor said, "My mom is my best friend … I respect her so much."[12]

Surrounded by Christmas

When Scott and Andrea were first married, they bought a Christmas tree farm in Wyomissing, intending to raise a family in a quiet, peaceful area. In addition to Scott's career in finance, the Swift family ran a side business growing and selling Christmas trees from their farm. Taylor cherishes her memories of her childhood. "I know that a Christmas tree farm in Pennsylvania is about the most random place for a country singer to come from," she has admitted. "But I had an awesome childhood. We had horses and cats, and my mom stayed home with me. Our dad would come home from work and then go outside to make a split-rail fence."[1] Growing up on that farm made her love the holiday celebrated near her birthday. She once said, "I think the fact that I love [Christmas] so much is probably because I grew up on a Christmas tree farm."[2] The Swift family spent their days surrounded by the Christmas spirit, which was a special experience for young Taylor.

1. Quoted in Rory Evans, "Interview with Taylor Swift: She's Living Her Taylor-Made Dream," *Women's Health*, December 2008. www.womenshealthmag.com/life/taylor-swift-interview.

2. Quoted in Tom Roland, "Justin Moore, Carrie Underwood: Christmas Time's a-Comin'," WRHI.com, December 23, 2010. www.wrhi.com/wrhm/2010/12/justin-moore-carrie-underwood-christmas-time's-a-comin'/.

Taylor's parents encouraged her to pursue her passions from an early age. When she was young, she wanted to ride horses, so her parents paid for riding lessons. Taylor even competed in horse shows as a child.

Taylor, shown here as a teenager, fell in love with country music at an early age.

A Love of Words

Taylor and Austin both attended elementary school at the private Wyndcroft School in nearby Pottstown, Pennsylvania. There,

Taylor excelled in English and creative writing. Taylor expressed her creativity from an early age through the written word, which helped her develop the storytelling abilities that would later show up in her songwriting. As a child, she loved to read poetry, and her favorites included Shel Silverstein poems. She also loved Dr. Seuss books. The poetry she read made a big impression on her, and she liked to replay the rhythm and rhyme of the words in her head. "I think I fell in love with words before I fell in love with music … All I wanted to do was talk and all I wanted to do was hear stories,"[13] she has said. Taylor's interest in poetry eventually inspired her to try her hand at writing some poems of her own.

Taylor began writing her own poetry when she was about 10 years old. She enjoyed the challenge of trying to find what she called "the perfect combination of words, with the perfect amount of syllables and the perfect rhyme."[14] She also loved putting words down on paper. While other kids in school dreaded poetry-writing assignments, Taylor felt energized by them and would turn in poems that were several pages long. When Taylor was in fourth grade, she won a national poetry contest for her poem "Monster in My Closet." This poem was three pages long, but it has never been released.

In addition to writing poetry, Taylor also wrote longer works of fiction. When she was 12, she wrote a novel over the summer that was more than 350 pages long. Like "Monster in My Closet," her novel has never been released publicly.

Born to Perform

Writing was not the only form of creative expression Taylor enjoyed as a child. Music was also a big part of her childhood. Growing up, Taylor loved to sing, and once she discovered LeAnn Rimes and other country music artists, Taylor could not stop singing songs from their albums.

Seeing her daughter's love of performing, Andrea encouraged Taylor to try out for the children's community theater in Wyomissing when she was about nine years old. Taylor loved

Musical Influences

Taylor was introduced to many different kinds of music as a child. Her maternal grandmother, Marjorie Finlay, was a professional opera singer and a member of the Houston Grand Opera. She had traveled all around the world to perform. Taylor considers her grandmother one of her biggest inspirations. Taylor's mother may have inherited her own mother's love of music, but she favored a much different style. Andrea was a fan of the heavy metal rock band Def Leppard and frequently played their albums at home. Country music also became a staple in the Swift household as Taylor grew up. When Taylor was six years old, she received country star LeAnn Rimes's album, *Blue*. Rimes, who was only 13 years old when the album was released, soon became a musical idol to Taylor. That album acted as a gateway for Taylor into the world of country music, and she then began listening to other leading ladies of country music, including Dolly Parton, Patsy Cline, and Shania Twain.

acting and performing in musicals. She was cast in the leading role of Sandy in the musical *Grease*. When she went onstage, she sang the musical's songs in a country music style. Taylor had been listening to country music for several years, so it felt natural to sing in that style. It was while performing in *Grease* that she made two important discoveries that would shape the rest of her life. One was that she loved being onstage and performing in front of a live audience with bright lights and applause. The other was that she wanted to become a country music singer.

From Coffeehouses to NBA Games

Taylor had made up her mind that she wanted to be the next big country music star. When she was about 10 years old, she began performing in public in Wyomissing, Reading, and other nearby towns in Pennsylvania. Taylor sang anywhere she could, including competitions, festivals, fairs, and coffeehouses. She also sang at karaoke nights in nearby restaurants, focusing on the country songs she already knew by heart. She even entered karaoke contests that were held in bars, although she had to beg her parents

Andrea (shown here) and Scott Swift always supported Taylor's big dreams and worked to help her make them a reality.

to let her do so. Scott and Andrea Swift were somewhat embarrassed to take their 10-year-old daughter to sing in a smoky bar,

Tough Times for Taylor's Mom

On April 9, 2015, Taylor wrote a post on her official Tumblr page to share some very difficult personal news with her fans: Her mother had been diagnosed with cancer. In that post, Taylor revealed the reason why Andrea was willing to let her share this news with her fans:

> She wanted you to know because your parents may be too busy juggling everything they've got going on to go to the doctor, and maybe you reminding them to go get checked for cancer could possibly lead to an early diagnosis and an easier battle ... Or peace of mind in knowing that they're healthy and there's nothing to worry about ... Thank you for caring about my family so much that she would want me to share this information with you. I hope and pray that you never get news like this.[1]

After sharing this post, Taylor and Andrea received well wishes from fans around the world. Cancer survivors and young people whose parents were battling the disease found inspiration in Andrea's fight and Taylor's honest words. Although the details of Andrea's condition have been kept private, she has been by her daughter's side for many of her most important milestones since her diagnosis and has appeared strong and happy.

1. Taylor Swift, "Just so you know...," Tumblr, April 9, 2015. taylorswift.tumblr.com/post/115942142045/just-so-you-know.

but they knew how much the chance to perform meant to Taylor.

One of Taylor's favorite places to perform was at the Pat Garrett Roadhouse in nearby Strausstown, Pennsylvania. Garrett is a country singer who sponsored karaoke contests at his roadhouse and gave the winner the opportunity to open for one of the country artists who performed at the Pat Garrett Amphitheater, which he also owned and operated. "I was in there every single week … I would go until I would win,"[15] Taylor said. It took Taylor a year—competing week after week—but at last her hard work and determination paid off. She won the chance to open for country music legend Charlie Daniels.

In addition to singing at karaoke contests, festivals, and fairs, Taylor also began singing "The Star Spangled Banner" at sporting events. She figured that without a record deal, this was the best way to get some exposure in front of large groups of people. One of her favorite experiences performing the national anthem was at a Philadelphia 76ers basketball game, because the famous rapper and hip-hop mogul Jay-Z was sitting in the audience. When she finished singing, he gave her a high five. "I bragged about that for like a year straight,"[16] Taylor said.

Feeling Like an Outsider

Although Taylor was receiving plenty of exposure and positive attention for her singing, country music was not a style of music that was popular where she lived. Her musical preferences and the fact that she was singing in public set her apart from the other kids in her neighborhood and at her school. This difference made her feel like an outsider, especially because the other kids made fun of her for liking country music.

One group of girls was especially hurtful to her. The girls teased her not only about her preference for country music but also about her appearance. These girls were popular, and they all had straight hair. Taylor had naturally curly hair, and in an effort to fit in better, she straightened her hair every morning—a time-consuming process that did not always work out well. "It looked so horrible—it completely frizzed out if it was humid outside, and it took me so long in the morning," Taylor recalled in an interview with *Allure* magazine in 2009. "But I suffered through that to try and be cool."[17] Taylor's efforts to fit in with the other girls did not seem to help matters. She explained, "They didn't think I was cool or pretty enough, so they stopped talking to me."[18] Taylor found being ostracized by her former friends very painful. She felt very isolated and lonely at school because the other girls did not include her in their conversations. She said that she would go to school "and not know who I was going to talk to. And that's a really terrifying thing for somebody who's 12."[19] Because of Taylor's personal experience with bullying, she has tried to give comfort and encouragement to kids and teenagers who are bullied. She has even reached out through social media to fans who have been bullied to send them personal messages of support.

Writing It Down

Fortunately for Taylor, she had a way to deal with the pain of being teased and ostracized. She threw herself into her music, trying to keep her spirits up despite her social troubles. On Friday nights, when the other girls would go to a sleepover she had not been invited to, she would sing karaoke in a restaurant or bar instead.

Soon, Taylor discovered another aspect of music that helped her process the confusion and loneliness of being rejected by her classmates. When she was 12 years old, a computer repairman named Ronnie—who was also an accomplished guitar player—taught her three chords on the guitar. She played the chords over and over until she had them just right. Then, she used those three chords to write her first song, which she called "Lucky You." Using those same three chords, she also wrote "The Outside," which is a song about the heartbreak and loneliness of feeling like she did not belong.

Taylor soon began to spend all her free time writing, playing,

Taylor learned to channel her negative feelings and experiences into music at a young age, which has inspired many of her young fans to find a creative outlet to deal with tough times in their own lives.

and singing her own songs. "I would write songs until my fingers bled, until my mother would make me leave my little computer room and come to dinner,"[20] she said. At first, her parents worried about their daughter because she was spending so much time alone. Andrea soon realized, however, that writing songs was Taylor's way of processing her feelings. Many of her songs dealt with themes of loneliness and being teased or bullied. "It's my way of coping," Taylor has said about her songwriting. "I write when I'm frustrated, angry, or confused. I've figured out a way to filter all of that into something good."[21] As it turns out, channeling her hurt and frustration into song lyrics would lead Taylor Swift to something very good, indeed.

Chapter Two

Dreams Come True in Nashville

Taylor Swift had big dreams of country music stardom. She also had the drive to achieve them. Taylor knew she needed to work hard to be successful, especially because she was so young. Some people in the music industry did not want to take her seriously because of her age. However, she did not let their lack of respect or the rejection she faced keep her from making her own music on her terms. Her determination paid off when she found a team of people who believed in her abilities and a new city to call home. In Nashville, Tennessee, Taylor's dreams finally came true.

The First Visit

Even before Taylor took up the guitar seriously, she had set her musical sights beyond Pennsylvania. When she was 11 years old, she watched a TV special on country music singer Faith Hill, whose music Taylor adored. Taylor learned from the show that the country star left school when she was 19 years old to pursue her dream of becoming a singer by moving to Nashville. This city is not only the capital of the state of Tennessee, it is also the

Taylor Swift credits Faith Hill with being one of her first mentors. She toured with the country music legend and her husband, Tim McGraw, in 2007. In an interview with the magazine *Glamour UK*, Taylor described Faith as "one of the first women to reach out to me and make me feel I had a friend in the music world."[22]

capital of the country music industry, and its nickname is "Music City." Nashville is home to several well-known venues for entertainers, including the Ryman Auditorium, the Grand Ole Opry House, Tootsie's Orchid Lounge, and the Bluebird Café. Many of Taylor's favorite country music singers got their start in Nashville.

After watching the special on Faith Hill, Taylor decided she also wanted to go to Nashville to get a recording contract. She made a recording of herself singing and begged her mother to take her there. Andrea agreed, and that spring break, she rented a car and took Taylor and Austin on a trip to Nashville. There, they drove up and down Music Row, which is the area of downtown Nashville that contains the offices of many businesses related to the music industry. Taylor would leave her mother and brother in the car while she walked into the offices of the record labels on Music Row. She then handed out her homemade demo CD to the receptionists. It took a lot of self-confidence for an 11-year-old to do that by herself.

During their trip to Nashville, Taylor's mother was very supportive, but she wanted her daughter to manage her expectations. As it turned out, Andrea's caution was warranted, because Taylor returned home to Wyomissing at the end of the week without a recording contract. In spite of this disappointment, Taylor remained determined to get a contract and become the next big country music singer.

A "Rising Star"

After her disappointing trip to Nashville, Taylor continued to sing at festivals, fairs, karaoke contests, and sporting events in and around Wyomissing. She also continued to play guitar and write songs. She realized that writing her own songs could make her stand out from the hundreds of other hopeful singers. She made more demo CDs, and her family began to visit Nashville regularly so she could hand out her demo to record labels.

Taylor's first big break came when she was asked by the U.S. Tennis Association to sing "The Star Spangled Banner" at the nationally televised U.S. Open tennis tournament in New York City. Taylor didn't know it at the time, but sitting in the audience that day was Dan Dymtrow, who was the manager of pop singer Britney Spears. He was so impressed by Taylor's singing that he asked her and her father to visit him in his office. Taylor took along her guitar and played some of her songs for him. After hearing her perform, Dymtrow agreed to be her manager.

Dymtrow lost no time promoting his newest singer. One of the first things he did was get her featured in clothing store Abercrombie & Fitch's "Rising Stars" advertising campaign. Dymtrow also had her record a new demo CD. Rather than singing along to prerecorded music, on this demo, Taylor accompanied herself on the guitar and sang songs she had written. Dymtrow also began spreading the word to those in the industry about his latest musical talent.

Changing for the Better

Dymtrow, who was well-known around the country as a promoter and manager, handed out Taylor's new demo to music label representatives in Nashville. His clout in the music industry, as well as the buzz he had already created surrounding Taylor, helped get music executives to listen to the CD. The executives were impressed by the talented young newcomer. Several of them told Dymtrow they wanted to hear her perform live. When Taylor next visited Nashville, she met with executives from several different labels on Music Row.

Taylor was thrilled when, in 2003, RCA Records offered her a one-year artist development deal. This means that the company agreed to provide her with studio time and resources to allow her to write and record music, but gave no promises that it would release an album. A development deal is not the same thing as an actual record deal, but it was a start. Taylor was overjoyed by this opportunity. At last, all her hard work was beginning to get her somewhere.

It was during this year that the Swift family made a decision that added to the positivity in Taylor's life. Commuting back and forth from Wyomissing to Nashville was difficult for Taylor and the rest of the family, so the Swifts moved to Nashville to support Taylor in her pursuit of a music career. The Swifts chose to live in a big house overlooking a lake in Hendersonville, which is a Nashville suburb. The scenic suburb was also the home of many country music singers, including Roy Orbison, Johnny Cash, and June Carter Cash.

The move to Hendersonville was helpful to Taylor in another way as well. She had been very unhappy in school back in Wyomissing, but at Hendersonville High School, she fit in much better with the other kids. Taylor also began to feel more comfortable about her appearance. She had already reached her full height of 5 feet 11 inches (180 cm) by this time. She also stopped straightening her hair and allowed it to curl naturally. The boys of Hendersonville High School began to take notice of her, and she began dating. These teenage romantic relationships inspired Taylor as she continued to write songs about her life.

Songwriting Skills

Although things were going well for Taylor in her personal life, they were not going quite the way she wanted at RCA. The record label's executives were not willing to produce an album of her songs. When they wanted her to record an album of other people's songs instead of her own, Taylor rejected the idea. "I didn't want to just be another girl singer. I wanted there to be something that set me apart. And I knew that had to be my writing,"[23] she explained in a 2007 interview with *Entertainment Weekly*. After a year of working on the development deal, she walked away from RCA and started looking for a new label. It was a bold move for her to make, but she would not settle for anything less than releasing an album full of her own songs. She also left her manager, Dan Dymtrow, at this time, and Scott Swift took over as her manager instead.

Taylor met with executives from several different labels, but

Taylor's Best Friend

Taylor Swift has many famous friends, but one of her closest friends is a girl she first met in English class at Hendersonville High School named Abigail Anderson. After that first meeting, they soon became best friends, and their friendship did a lot to help Taylor feel more comfortable at Hendersonville High School than she ever did in junior high in Wyomissing. Although the two young women followed different paths—with Abigail attending the University of Kansas to compete on their swim team—they have remained best friends. In fact, Taylor wrote about Abigail in her hit song "Fifteen" from her 2008 album *Fearless*. Abigail even went as Taylor's date to the 2015 Grammy Awards.

each one was reluctant to give a recording contract to someone so young. Taylor knew, however, that county music greats LeAnn Rimes and Tanya Tucker had both debuted at 13 years old, and she was determined not to let her own young age stand in her way. She kept talking to various labels until she finally found one that was interested in her. Sony/ATV Music Publishing was impressed by her songwriting talent, and they gave her a publishing deal as a house writer. She became the youngest person the record label had ever signed as a songwriter. Taylor was partnered with older, more experienced writers, which is a technique the music industry commonly uses to mentor up-and-coming songwriters. This was a little intimidating for her at first. "I walked into writers' session with writers that I knew were hit songwrit-

Friendship is important to Taylor, and she still considers Abigail Anderson one of her closest friends. Abigail's friendship has meant a lot to Taylor over the years, especially after the loneliness she felt in Wyomissing.

ers," she said. "I knew they were going to have serious doubts about walking in and working with [me]."[24] It was up to Taylor to change their minds with her maturity and talent.

The pressure was on, but Taylor handled it gracefully. She approached her job with a professional attitude, and she arrived at each writing session with as many as 20 ideas for songs ready to go. She got many of her ideas throughout the day while she was in school. "I knew that I had to work just as hard as the veteran 45-year-old writers,"[25] Taylor said. Her co-writers were impressed with her dedication and skills, and she soon earned the respect of other songwriters in Nashville. Country music singer, songwriter, and producer John Rich said of Taylor, "You can hear great pop sensibilities in her writing as well as great storytelling, which is the trademark of old-school country song-crafting."[26]

One of the veteran songwriters Taylor was paired with was a woman named Liz Rose. The two of them clicked immediately. They worked together once a week after Taylor got out of school, and Rose had high praise for the teenager's skill and talent. "She's a genius, coming in with ideas and a melody," Rose said. "I never second-guessed her. I respect her a lot."[27] The feeling was entirely mutual. In a 2007 interview, Taylor said, "I love writing with Liz."[28] Under Liz Rose's guidance, Taylor became a more polished songwriter and channeled her high school experiences into what would become her first hit songs.

Some song ideas Taylor came up with were intended for other artists. Most of the songs, however, were meant for Taylor to record. Sony allowed her to keep those songs for herself. She wanted to have a collection of songs ready for the day that she finally secured a record deal.

A Record Deal

Soon, Taylor had written more than enough songs that she was able to fill an album. The problem was, she still did not have a record deal. She had hoped Sony would offer her a recording contract, but the company had not offered her one. She recorded new demo CDs of her songs with a producer named Nathan Chapman, who also played instruments for the recordings. Taylor shopped these new demos around at other labels. She also continued to perform in public every chance she could, just as she had back in Wyomissing.

One of these performances turned out to be extremely important for her career. One night in 2004, Taylor was showcased at the Bluebird Café in Nashville. This famed café features up-and-coming artists, and the venue played a part in launching several high-profile country music careers. Taylor was the youngest performer that night. She sang a set of her own songs, including "Picture to Burn."

Sitting in the audience when Taylor performed that night

was music executive Scott Borchetta of DreamWorks Records. Borchetta, who was a 20-year veteran of the music industry, had heard Taylor's demo and was so impressed by her singing and songwriting that he came down to see her perform live at the Bluebird Café. What he saw that night convinced him to sign Taylor immediately to a record deal.

The record deal Borchetta offered Taylor, however, was not with DreamWorks. He had decided to leave that label and form one of his own, which would be called Big Machine Records. Borchetta wanted Taylor to be the first artist he signed. Others in the industry may have been worried about signing someone so young, but Borchetta saw past Taylor's youth; in fact, he said, "It never hit me that Taylor was a teenager. To me, she was a hit songwriter."[29] Taylor finally found someone who believed in her as a singer and songwriter enough to give her the record deal she'd worked so hard to secure.

"Tim McGraw"

Taylor was overjoyed to have a recording contract at last, and she was honored and excited to be a part of Borchetta's new venture. They got to work right away recording an album. They selected three songs she wrote herself and eight she wrote with others, including Liz Rose. Titled *Taylor Swift*, the album took four months to complete. At first, Taylor experimented with several different producers but she was not happy with the way the tracks sounded. Finally, she and Borchetta decided to use Nathan Chapman. Though Chapman had produced her demo CDs, he was not their first pick because he had never produced an album before. Chapman wound up producing all but one of the singles for the album, and he played several instruments on the album, as he had done for her demo.

One of the songs selected for the album was "Tim McGraw," which was among the first songs Taylor and Rose had worked on together. When Taylor played "Tim McGraw" for Borchetta, he liked it so much he chose it to be the first single. Even before

Singing at the Bluebird

The Bluebird Café, which opened in Nashville in 1982, hosts both famous singer/songwriters and those who hope to follow in their footsteps. The club was opened by Amy Kurland, who envisioned a café in which customers could hear music while dining. At first, performers appeared only occasionally, but as more customers discovered the Bluebird, live music became a regular attraction. Among the famous artists who got their start at the Bluebird are Garth Brooks and Taylor Swift.

In July 1984, the café held its first weekly Writer's Night, in which new songwriters get the chance to play their own material with established performers. The first guest was Don Schlitz, who won a Grammy Award for writing Kenny Rogers's hit song "The Gambler," which was released in 1978. The Bluebird also hosts dinner shows and weekly open mic nights.

In 2002, the Bluebird received an Academy of Country Music Award for Night Club of the Year. In 2008, founder and owner Kurland transferred ownership of the Bluebird to the Nashville Songwriters Association International as a way to continue the café's commitment to songwriters and the community. The Bluebird Café is such an important part of the Nashville music

the song's release, Taylor began promoting it—and her upcoming album—on the social networking website MySpace. She created a profile for herself as a country music artist, wrote a biography that was posted on her profile, and embedded all of the tracks from her album on her page. She included photos and video clips of herself, a link to her official website, and a schedule

scene that it became a prominent setting on the television show *Nashville*, which premiered in 2012.

The Bluebird Café, shown here, is famous for launching the careers of some of the biggest names in country music, including Taylor Swift.

of promotional events. Thousands of fans began viewing this page and downloading "Tim McGraw" and other songs from her first album.

"Tim McGraw" stayed on *Billboard* magazine's Hot Country Songs chart for 35 weeks, peaking at number 6. It also appeared on the Billboard Hot 100 chart, reaching number 40. The song,

"Tim McGraw" showed that Taylor Swift was a new kind of country artist who could connect to the feelings and experiences of teenage girls in a meaningful and marketable way.

The Story Behind the Song

Like many of Taylor Swift's songs, "Tim McGraw" was inspired by one of her relationships. She wrote the song after spending time thinking about the fact that her high school boyfriend would be graduating and leaving her behind to go off to college. The song's title refers to the couple's favorite song, "Can't Tell Me Nothin'" by Tim McGraw. Taylor's producer, Nathan Chapman, described "Tim McGraw" as "such a different way of talking about love between two people."[1] This unique approach to singing about young love made Taylor stand out from the pack of other country artists, and the personal feel of her first single influenced every song she's released after it.

1. Quoted in Will Robinson, "Taylor Swift's First Producer Looks Back on 'Tim McGraw' 10 Years Later," *Entertainment Weekly*, June 19, 2016. www.ew.com/article/2016/06/19/taylor-swift-tim-mcgraw-turns-10.

which would go on to win an award for Breakthrough Video of the Year at the 2007 CMT Music Awards, created a lot of buzz for Taylor's upcoming album. Another thing creating buzz was the fact that she had written or helped write all the songs on the album—an unusual accomplishment for any first album, let alone for someone so young. At 16 years old, Taylor Swift was poised to take the country music industry by storm.

Chapter **Three**

Superstar Status

In the span of only six years—from 2006 to 2012—Taylor Swift released four albums: *Taylor Swift, Fearless, Speak Now,* and *Red.* They all topped the country music charts and made her the country superstar she dreamed of becoming when she was a little girl in Wyomissing. As Swift grew up with each album she released, she became more and more of a crossover star whose catchy and confessional songs appealed to pop music fans, too.

Chart-Topping Debut

While "Tim McGraw" soared to the top of the charts during the summer of 2006, Taylor Swift's fans eagerly awaited the release of her album. As soon as school let out for the summer, Swift embarked on a radio tour to promote the lead single and the album. She visited radio stations across the country to give interviews and perform the hit song. Most radio tours last six weeks, but Swift's lasted six months. "I wanted to meet every single one of the people that was helping me out,"[30] she explained in a December 2006 interview with Country Music Television (CMT). Her MySpace page received more than 2 million hits before her first album was finally released on October 24, 2006.

Taylor Swift quickly lived up to the hype generated by "Tim McGraw," Swift's following on social media, and her radio tour. The album sold 39,000 copies in its first week. It debuted on the Billboard 200 albums chart at number 19 and peaked at number 5. *Taylor Swift* reached number 1 on the Billboard Top Country Albums chart, and by June 2007, it was certified platinum by the Recording Industry Association of America (RIAA), having sold 1 million copies. It would eventually be certified 5 times platinum for selling more than 5 million copies. Swift made history by becoming the first female country artist to write or co-write every song on a platinum-selling album.

More tracks were released as singles after the album came out. The second single, "Teardrops on My Guitar," was released in February 2007 and peaked at number 2 on the Billboard Hot Country Songs chart. It also crossed over to the pop charts, reaching number 13 on the Billboard Hot 100, and the video for the song played on cable music networks MTV and VH1. Taylor Swift's name was now familiar to millions of country and pop music fans alike.

The third single, "Our Song," spent six weeks at number 1 on the Hot Country Songs chart and peaked at number 16 on the Billboard Hot 100. The fourth single from her album was "Picture to Burn," which she had played that fateful night at the Bluebird Café when Borchetta was in the audience. Swift's life had already changed so much from the night she first played that song at the Bluebird. She was no longer an aspiring country singer; she had become a true country star with huge crossover appeal.

Life on the Road

Shortly after the release of her runaway hit debut album, Swift

Swift spent much of the year following the release of her debut album touring with famous country musicians.

received invitations to tour with other artists. First, the country trio Rascal Flatts invited her to open for nine shows on their tour. She had only two days' notice before she hit the road with the group, but she was excited to go on a concert tour for the first time and perform in front of such large audiences.

Swift learned a lot from touring with Rascal Flatts, and soon had many chances to put that knowledge to use. Soon after her tour with the trio ended, country music singer George Strait invited her to open for his tour, which he headlined with country music legend Ronnie Milsap. Swift toured with them for more than two months. Next, Swift was invited to tour with country music singer Brad Paisley. Swift spent about five months touring with Paisley and several other artists, including Rodney Atkins, Jack Ingram, Kellie Pickler, and Chuck Wicks. Swift and Pickler, who rose to fame on the TV show *American Idol*, became good friends during the tour. They wrote a song together during that time that became Pickler's 2009 single "Best Days of Your Life."

In the summer of 2007, Swift received one of the biggest thrills of her life when she was invited to open for Tim McGraw and Faith Hill on their *Soul2Soul II* tour. Not only did McGraw's name

Early EPs

Before releasing a second album or embarking on her own tour, Swift released two extended play, or EP, albums. One was a 2007 holiday album titled *Sounds of the Season: The Taylor Swift Holiday Collection*. The EP was released exclusively at Target and contained six songs. Most of them were covers of traditional holiday songs, with two original songs also included.

Swift's other EP, titled *Beautiful Eyes*, was released in the summer of 2008 as a limited release available only at Wal-Mart stores and the Wal-Mart website. The EP, which also contained only six songs, sold 45,000 copies in its first week. Three cuts are alternate versions of songs from her first album: "Should've Said No," "Teardrops on My Guitar," and "Picture to Burn." The EP included two new songs, "Beautiful Eyes" and "I Heart ?," both of which Swift wrote. *Beautiful Eyes* also included a DVD that contained music videos and performances by Swift. This EP was not heavily promoted because Swift did not want her fans to confuse it for her second album, which was released shortly after *Beautiful Eyes*.

serve as the title of Swift's first big hit, but Hill had been one of Swift's role models and a big influence on her singing and song-writing. Being invited to tour with them was a dream come true.

Swift was invited to tour again with Rascal Flatts in 2008. Her mother accompanied her on the road during all the tours. Her father stayed home with her younger brother, Austin. By the end of the second tour with Rascal Flatts, Swift had been touring for almost an entire year.

The hectic pace gave Swift the opportunity to hone her performance skills. She learned a lot from her tour mates about the details of handling a tour and interacting with a large audience. During this busy year, Swift continued to write songs and was already thinking about and planning a second album.

A Fearless *Year*

Fans did not have to wait long for Swift's second album, *Fearless*. Released in November 2008, it debuted at number 1 on the Billboard 200 chart and the Top Country Albums chart, and it sold more than 592,300 copies in the United States in its first week, which was the best first-week performance for any female artist that year. In addition, it was the highest-selling album of 2009 in any genre. To date, *Fearless* has sold more than 7 million copies in the United States alone.

As she did on her first album, Swift wrote or co-wrote all the songs on *Fearless*. Several singles were released from the album, including "Love Story," "White Horse," and "You Belong with Me." A sure sign of her influence on popular culture is the fact that, around this time, her songs began to show up on hit TV shows. For example, "White Horse" was featured in the season premiere of one of Swift's favorite shows, *Grey's Anatomy*, in the fall of 2008.

The lead single, "Love Story," which Swift said she wrote in just 20 minutes on the floor of her bedroom, became the biggest hit from the album. Within a year, "Love Story" had been downloaded more than 3 million times, which was the most paid downloads of any song in history at that time. It has sold more than 8 million copies worldwide since its release. The song reached number 4 on the Billboard Hot 100 and went on to be certified 5 times platinum by the RIAA.

Critics generally gave *Fearless* positive reviews, saying that Swift's lyrics showed maturity beyond her years. Jody Rosen, a reviewer for *Rolling Stone* magazine, wrote that this album showed that Swift had "an intuitive gift"[31] for structuring her songs in a memorable way. Some critics were less enthusiastic about Swift's performances, however, complaining that her voice was thin and unexpressive when she performed live.

Swift's second album was a critical and commercial success that earned her many awards, including four Grammy Awards.

Taylor vs. Kanye

At the MTV Video Music Awards (VMAs) on the night of September 13, 2009, Swift won the award for Best Female Video for "You Belong with Me." During her acceptance speech, rapper Kanye West walked onstage and took the microphone away from her. While Swift stood by, West announced, "Taylor, I'm really happy for you and I'mma let you finish, but Beyoncé had one of the best videos of all time."[1] West was referring to singer Beyoncé Knowles's video for "Single Ladies (Put a Ring on It)," which had been nominated for Best Female Video along with Swift's video. West left the stage almost as quickly as he had arrived, but the embarrassed Swift was unable to finish her acceptance speech properly, only uttering a handful of words to thank her fans and MTV.

Later in the evening, when Beyoncé won the Best Video of the Year Award for "Single Ladies (Put a Ring on It)," she walked onto the stage and announced, "I would like Taylor to come out and have her moment."[2] By this time, Swift had regained her composure. She accepted the microphone and completed her acceptance speech.

This was not the last interaction between Swift and West. Although they appeared to have made amends—with Swift even presenting the rapper with the Video Vanguard Award at the 2015 VMAs—they publicly feuded once again over Swift's inclusion in West's 2016 song, "Famous," in which he claimed he made Swift famous and called her an offensive term for a woman. While Swift denied giving West permission to use her name in his song, his wife, Kim Kardashian, released videos in July 2016 that appeared to feature Swift doing exactly that in a recorded phone call. Swift then took to Instagram to clarify that she never heard the song and did not know he would be calling her an offensive name in it. Several years after their first encounter at the VMAs, it seemed this conflict was far from over.

1. Quoted in 2009 MTV Video Music Awards, MTV, September 13, 2009.

2. Quoted in 2009 MTV Video Music Awards.

West and Swift at the 2009 VMAs

More awards and nominations came Swift's way with *Fearless*. These included American Music Awards for Artist of the Year and Favorite Country Album, as well as a Country Music Association Award for Album of the Year. In addition, she won an Academy of Country Music Award for Album of the Year.

She was also nominated for a total of eight Grammy Awards. Swift, who had been disappointed at the Grammy Awards two years earlier after she came home empty-handed, did not expect to win any this time around and told an interviewer from *Rolling Stone*, "I'm a really, really happy person, thinking about being nominated for eight of them, and I think that's a gift in itself."[32] She did win, however, taking home a total of four Grammy Awards in 2010: Best Female Country Vocal Performance and Best Country Song for "White Horse," as well as Best Country Album and Album of the Year for *Fearless*. At only 20 years old, Swift became the youngest artist in the history of the Grammy Awards to take home the prize for Album of the Year.

On the Road Again

In April 2009, Swift kicked off her first solo tour. Before the tour, she and her band practiced for three weeks in a secret warehouse in Nashville. Swift was involved in every aspect of the tour, including the design of the stage, which featured a hidden elevator for the performers to move to and from the stage.

The *Fearless* tour traveled to more than 50 cities in the United States and Canada. The massive, sold-out tour included opening performances by musical groups Gloriana and Molo Eight. Kellie Pickler also opened for Swift on the tour. Other guest performers included Faith Hill, John Mayer, and Katy Perry.

The *Fearless* tour was originally scheduled to end in late November 2009, but ticket demand was so high that Swift expanded it into the next year. Fellow teenage singer Justin Bieber joined her on her tour in the United Kingdom, where Swift played concerts in several cities, including London and Manchester. Swift then flew to Australia, where she performed in

Famous Guests

Taylor Swift has become known for the famous guests she performs with during her tours. After featuring Katy Perry, John Mayer, and other artists during her *Fearless* tour, she continued to add more celebrity appearances to her sets. In 2013, Jennifer Lopez joined Swift on stage for a performance in Los Angeles, California, during Swift's *Red* tour. When Swift went on tour in 2015 to promote her hit album *1989*, a parade of famous faces were seen performing with her. The *1989* tour featured musicians who were popular with young people, such as Lorde, Shawn Mendes, Ellie Goulding, and Justin Timberlake. It also featured appearances by music legends, such as Mick Jagger, Mary J. Blige, and Steven Tyler. Swift even had celebrities not known for their musical talents, such as Dwyane Wade, Julia Roberts, and Ellen DeGeneres, share the stage with her. In one of the most memorable moments from that tour, Swift sang a duet with Lisa Kudrow, who appeared as her character Phoebe Buffay from the TV show *Friends*. The two sang the song "Smelly Cat" from that hit show.

Brisbane, Sydney, and other cities. Her tour continued through the United States and Canada until June 2010. Swift was enormously pleased by the sold-out concerts and the enthusiasm of the crowds. "It's the most amazing feeling," she said in a 2009 interview. "It's one of the craziest feelings to be on stage and know that you were sitting on your bedroom floor when that song came to be and now there's an arena full of people singing it."[33]

"An Enormous Breakthrough"

While on the *Fearless* tour, Swift kept busy writing new songs for her third album. *Speak Now* was released in October 2010 and debuted at number 1 on the Billboard 200. The album sold more than 1 million copies in the United States during its first week—outselling any other release on the charts at the time by far. The album has been certified quadruple platinum by the RIAA for selling more than 4 million copies since its release.

Swift wrote all 14 of the songs on *Speak Now* herself. In November 2010, 11 of those songs were featured on the Billboard Hot 100 chart. That set a record for the most songs by a female artist on the Hot 100 at one time. Swift held that record until Beyoncé broke it in 2016.

Overall, music critics were impressed by the album. Chris Willman of the *Hollywood Reporter* called it "an enormous breakthrough in songwriting maturity."[34] Another critic, Elysa Gardner, wrote in *USA Today* that the album "captures the sweet ache of becoming an adult, as only those who are still in the process can articulate."[35]

However, some critics and listeners seemed to focus only on who Swift's songs—including "Dear John" and "Back to December"—were about. Swift's songwriting had always come from personal experiences, but *Speak Now* was when the attention given to which personal experiences inspired which lyrics went into overdrive. People speculated at length about Swift's love life (including her rumored romances with John Mayer and *Twilight* star Taylor Lautner) and how it was reflected in her *Speak Now* songs. The speculation was fueled by the fact that Swift never revealed who the songs were really about. Although that kind of attention took some of the focus away from the music itself, it was not all bad for Swift. In fact, Emily Yahr of the *Washington Post* called it "a brilliant strategy" and wrote, "The guessing game helped her turn every album release into a frenzy."[36] The "frenzy" surrounding the release of *Speak Now* certainly had a lot to do with the unnamed inspirations for some of the album's best songs.

Taylor Swift's successful 2010 was capped off by an inclusion on *TIME* magazine's list of the 100 most influential people in the world.

Speak Now won many awards, too. Swift was nominated for four 2011 Academy of Country Music Awards, including Female Vocalist of the Year, Entertainer of the Year, and Album of the

Year (as both artist and producer) for *Speak Now*. Swift won Entertainer of the Year, which was especially meaningful to her because the viewers vote for the winner. "This is the first time I've ever won this, and I'm losing my mind!" Swift proclaimed in her acceptance speech. "The fact that this was from the fans is so beautiful. You are the best thing that has ever happened to me."[37] Swift also won two Grammy Awards for the song "Mean" from the album: Best Country Solo Performance and Best Country song.

In November 2010, Swift announced that she would be traveling the world on the *Speak Now* tour throughout the following year. The tour took her to South Korea, Japan, France, Italy, and many other countries she'd never performed in before. Closer to home, Swift played in some of the biggest stadiums in the United States, including Cowboys Stadium in Dallas, Texas.

Seeing Red

On October 22, 2012, Swift released her fourth album, *Red*. In the first week, it sold 1.21 million copies, which was the most successful first week for an album in a decade. With those impressive sales, *Red* debuted at number 1 on the Billboard 200 chart. Its lead single, "We Are Never Ever Getting Back Together," became the first single in Swift's career to reach number 1 on the Billboard Hot 100 chart.

Red was unlike anything Swift had ever done before. As its success on the Hot 100 chart showed, "We Are Never Ever Getting Back Together" was a pop song, and Swift was clearly crossing into pop music territory on many of *Red*'s tracks. *Billboard* magazine called the album "Taylor Swift's first adult pop album."[38] It marked the real beginning of her transition from country star to pop star. In fact, *New York Times* critic Jon Caramanica called the pop songs on *Red* "among the best songs on this album."[39] *Red* was seen as a bridge album by many—between country and pop, as well as between innocence and adulthood in Swift's songwriting. It was generally received well by critics and fans, with *Billboard* calling it "her most interesting full-length to date"[40] when

Red gave Swift's fans their first real taste of the pop music she would create as her career took a new and exciting turn.

it reviewed the album in 2012.

As of 2016, *Red* has sold more than 4 million copies—another quadruple-platinum success for Swift. That success carried over into Swift's *Red* tour, which took the singer to four continents in 15 months. The tour sold over 1.7 million tickets to earn more than $150 million, which broke the record for a solo tour by a country artist. Swift played in huge stadiums and arenas on the *Red* tour, proving her superstar status at the box office.

Chapter **Four**

The Next Chapter

A new chapter in Swift's life began in 2014. She started the year with a move to a new city, which hinted at the new direction her music was about to take. Swift had always been a country singer with huge crossover appeal, but now she felt ready to take a big step away from country music and into the pop music spotlight. By leaving Nashville behind for the bright lights of New York City, Swift's career entered uncharted territory. It was a risky move for Swift to leave the comforts of country music behind, but it was a risk that paid off.

Welcome to New York

In early 2014, Swift moved into a large penthouse apartment in the Tribeca neighborhood of New York City. Swift fully embraced the unique energy of New York City, and she treated the move as an important moment in her journey toward becoming more self-aware as an artist and as a young woman. In a letter to her fans that was posted on her official website on October 27, 2014, Swift wrote, "I think you have to know who you are and what you want in order to take on New York in all its blaring truth."[41]

Swift's enthusiasm for New York City inspired the city's official tourism and marketing organization, NYC & Company, to name her a Global Welcome Ambassador for tourism.

At Home with Taylor Swift

In addition to Swift's Tribeca penthouse, she has a penthouse apartment in Nashville, which is not far from the large home she reportedly purchased for her parents. Swift also has a home in Beverly Hills, California, and an oceanfront house in Rhode Island. At home, Swift loves to entertain, and she famously enjoys baking.

Swift's Watch Hill, Rhode Island, mansion is best known as the site of some of her most famous Fourth of July parties, which she and her friends document on Instagram and other forms of social media. However, Swift did not immediately make friends with her neighbors in this exclusive community. When she rebuilt the home's seawall, her neighbors accused her of ruining the shoreline. The controversy did not stop Swift from dubbing her Rhode Island home "her 'dream house,'"[1] according to a 2014 interview with *Rolling Stone*.

No matter where Swift is living, security is incredibly important to her. When she bought her Tribeca penthouse, she also bought the unit across the hall for her security team to live in because she wanted to keep them close. Because so much of her life has been lived in the public eye, Swift carefully guards her privacy at home, and having a security team close by is a comfort to her.

1. Josh Eells, "The Reinvention of Taylor Swift," *Rolling Stone*, September 8, 2014. www.rolling-stone.com/music/features/taylor-swift-1989-cover-story-20140908.

By 2014, Swift felt she knew who she was and what she wanted, and both of those things were different than anything she had shown the world before.

Around the time Swift moved to New York City, she debuted

a new shorter haircut, which was a big departure from her previous style. In fact, she wrote that she had always been "the girl who said she would never cut her hair."[42] The unprecedented change in her personal style was a sign that Swift was beginning to reinvent herself. Her look and her address had changed, and it seemed her music was about to change, too.

Swift Shakes It Off

On August 18, 2014, Swift hosted a live-stream on the popular website Yahoo! to give her fans a taste of the new music she had been working on since the release of *Red*. During that live-stream, Swift made the major announcement that she was going to be releasing her first purely pop album. She also showed her fans the album's cover and revealed its title: *1989*. The album title referenced the year Swift was born and the music that inspired its creation. As Swift said, "I was listening to a lot of late-Eighties pop. I really love the chances they were taking. I love how bold it was. I love how ahead of its time it was … It was apparently a time of just limitless potential."[43] Swift felt that same sense of "limitless potential" in her own life at the time she was working on *1989*, especially after her move to New York City. She wanted her music to reflect what she was feeling, and pop music seemed to be the best fit at this stage of her life.

In addition to revealing basic details about *1989*, Swift also used her Yahoo! live-steam to release the music video for the album's first single, "Shake It Off." The song instantly became a huge hit, with its catchy hook and message of ignoring the people who want to bring you down. It reached number 1 on the Billboard Hot 100 chart and has sold more than 8 million copies to become certified 8 times platinum.

"Shake It Off" was nominated for three Grammy Awards in 2015, even though the rest of *1989* was not eligible for the Grammys until the following year. The song was nominated for Record of the Year, Song of the Year, and Best Pop Solo Performance.

"Secret Sessions"

With the success of "Shake It Off," the prerelease buzz around *1989* was already louder than it had been for any of Swift's previous albums. In order to keep specifics about the album secret and to keep tracks or any other information from being leaked, Swift increased the already tight security around her. For example, during the music video shoot for "Shake It Off," a reporter for *Rolling Stone* wrote, "Every doorway and stairwell is guarded, and every window is blacked out."[44] Swift also kept all the songs from the album locked away on her phone.

Although Swift carefully protected her new album, she still wanted some of her most devoted fans to hear it before it was released. Many artists host listening parties in big cities where they play tracks from upcoming albums for fans. Swift took it one big step further—and one step closer to her fans. She and her team scoured social media for passionate fans to invite to her Nashville, New York, Rhode Island, and California homes, as well as a property in London in the United Kingdom. Swift then met with those small groups of fans and played the songs from *1989* for them. She also baked them cookies, which added to the atmosphere she described to the *Los Angeles Times*: "It feels like a party, or a sleepover."[45] These intimate listening parties were named the "Secret Sessions," and they helped strengthen the connection between the singer and her fans during a period of transition in her career—a time when she could have alienated fans who came to care about her first as a country music artist.

The "Secret Sessions" reminded fans that the personal touch Swift was famous for in both her music and fan interactions was not going to disappear just because she was now exclusively making pop music. The fans who were chosen to experience these sessions responded positively to the album they heard. One 21-year-old fan told the *Los Angeles Times* during Swift's California "Secret Session," "I've been a fan since I was 14. She's never disappointed me."[46]

1989 *Tops the Charts*

The rest of the world finally got to hear what Swift's fans heard during her "Secret Sessions" on October 27, 2014, when *1989* was released. The album was an immediate success, debuting at number 1 on the Billboard 200 chart. It sold 1.287 million copies

The way Swift's fans embraced *1989* meant a lot to her because the album was seen as such a gamble for her as an artist.

in its first week alone, which topped *Red*'s first-week sales to make it the highest-selling album in its first week since Eminem's 2002 album *The Eminem Show*. With that successful week at the top of the charts, Swift became the only artist since sales started being tracked in 1991 to have three albums sell more than 1 million copies in the span of a week: *Speak Now*, *Red*, and *1989*.

By July 2015, *1989* had sold more than 5 million copies to become certified 5 times platinum. That was the fastest any album had sold 5 million copies in more than a decade. The album's success continued throughout that year. In November 2015, it celebrated a full year in the top 10 on the Billboard 200 chart. As of that date, it was only the fifth album ever to spend its entire first year among the top 10 albums.

A Different Direction

Much of the conversation around *1989* involved the word "different." Its style, its themes, and its lyrics were different from anything else Swift had done in her career. Questions about the shift from country music to pop music dominated the interviews Swift did to promote the album, and Swift explained that decision came from the fact that she felt she needed to make a choice between the country and pop music worlds she had been splitting her time between for much of her career. In an interview with *Billboard* magazine after the release of *1989*, she said, "It felt disingenuous to try to exploit two genres when your album only falls in one."[47] Swift wanted to be honest with both her team and her fans: She made a pop record and only a pop record. There was no attempt to blend country music into the sound of *1989*, and Swift understood what a risk that was after establishing herself as a country music star.

On the day of *1989*'s release, Swift defended her new style on her website: "I've woken up every day not wanting, but needing to write a new style of music. I needed to change the way I told my stories and the way they sounded."[48] Swift also explained that the stories she told on this album were different from the ones she had become famous for telling. As Swift explained in *Rolling Stone*, "It's not as boy-centric of an album, because my life hasn't been boycentric."[49] This album featured fewer songs about Swift's famous ex-boyfriends, which put some of the focus back on her music instead of the men who had inspired that music. As the *New York Times* review of the album stated, "While there are certainly references to some of Ms. Swift's high-profile relationships, the album on the whole feels less diaristic than her previous work."[50] This shift in the album's content away from personal accounts of romantic relationships and toward a broader look at life and love could have been a disaster for an artist who was famous for her personal lyrics. However, *1989* was anything but a disaster. Its huge sales figures proved that different was good for Swift.

A String of Hit Singles

"Shake It Off" was Swift's first hit single from *1989*, but it was far from her last. Her second single from the album was "Blank Space." On this track, Swift sings about her reputation for being a serial dater in what *Los Angeles Times* music critic Mikael Wood described as a "thrillingly vicious"[51] way. Other critics responded well to the song, too, with many calling it one of the best on the album. Jon Caramanica called the song, "Ms. Swift at her peak."[52] Fans also embraced this fun take on the rumor mill surrounding Swift's love life. "Blank Space" spent seven weeks at number 1 on the Billboard Hot 100 chart, and the music video for the song has been watched on YouTube more than 1.7 billion times as of 2016.

The third single from *1989* was "Style," which many critics praised when the album was first released. Caramanica called the song "the high mark"[53] of the album. Wood echoed Caramanica's opinion of this song. In his review of *1989*, he singled out "Style" for showing "a sense of grown-up emotion she's never fully embraced before."[54] The song was also a hit on the charts, climbing to number 6 on the Hot 100.

On May 17, 2015, the music video for Swift's next single,

Ryan Adams Sings
Taylor Swift

In September 2015, famous singer-songwriter Ryan Adams released a cover of *1989*. Adams recorded his own versions of the songs from Swift's album with the social media seal of approval from Swift, who tweeted enthusiastically about his project. Swift had admired Adams's music for many years, so she called the experience of having him cover her songs "surreal and dream-like."[1] Adams took Swift's songs and recorded them in his own style over the course of two weeks. During the recording sessions, Adams found himself sincerely connecting with Swift's songs. He told *Rolling Stone*, "As I was singing those songs, they mattered to me as much as any of my own songs ever did. Or I wouldn't have sung them."[2] Listeners responded favorably to Adams's take on Swift's music. His *1989* cover album debuted at number 7 on the Billboard 200 chart.

1. Quoted in Ian Crouch, "Haters Gonna Hate: Listening to Ryan Adams's '1989,'" *The New Yorker*, September 22, 2015. www.newyorker.com/culture/culture-desk/haters-gonna-hate-listening-to-ryan-adams-1989.

2. Quoted in David Browne, "Ryan Adams on His Full-Album Taylor Swift Cover: 'You Just Have to Mean It,'" *Rolling Stone*, September 21. 2015. www.rollingstone.com/music/news/ryan-adams-on-his-full-album-taylor-swift-cover-you-just-have-to-mean-it-20150921.

"Bad Blood," premiered during the Billboard Music Awards. The video featured rapper Kendrick Lamar, as well as some of the most famous women in entertainment, including many of Swift's closest friends. The video was a pop culture talking point for weeks—even being parodied on *Saturday Night Live*—and has nearly 1 billion views on YouTube as of 2016. The success of the

Ryan Adams

"Bad Blood" music video helped propel the song to the top of the Billboard Hot 100 chart.

Before the end of 2015, Swift saw another one of her songs crack the top 10 on the Hot 100. In November, "Wildest Dreams" reached number 5 on the chart. The next single from the album was "Out of the Woods," which details a mysterious accident that

As of 2016, five of Swift's singles from *1989* had spent time in the top 10 on the Billboard Hot 100 chart. That is the highest number of singles to do so from any of her albums up to that point.

landed Swift and her boyfriend at the time in the hospital. Swift chose to include such a personal anecdote in an album that had fewer of those than normal for her "to remind people that there are really big things they don't know about"[55] that have happened in her life. The song was first released in 2014 to promote the album, but it was officially released as a single in February 2016. "Out of the Woods" became Swift's sixth song from *1989* to land in the top 20 on the Billboard Pop Songs chart, and it peaked at number 12 on that chart. In April 2016, "New Romantics" also cracked the Pop Songs top 20, peaking at number 18.

"**Bad** Blood"

One of the most publicized tracks on *1989*—even before the album's release—was "Bad Blood." Like many of Swift's songs before it, "Bad Blood" was surrounded by a sea of speculation concerning whom the song was about. Unlike many other Swift songs, however, the speculation was not about a man. "Bad Blood" was actually about a feud between Swift and another female artist. Swift explained the feud in an interview with *Rolling Stone*:

> For years, I was never sure if we were friends or not ... [Then] she did something so horrible. I was like, 'Oh we're just straight-up enemies.' And it wasn't even about a guy! It had to do with business. She basically tried to sabotage an entire arena tour. She tried to hire a bunch of people out from under me.[1]

Based on the fact that some of Swift's dancers left her tour to join Katy Perry's tour, insiders and fans alike have come to the conclusion that "Bad Blood" is about Perry.

The music video for "Bad Blood" plays out this conflict between two powerful women like an action movie, with Swift training to battle her enemy. That enemy was played by Swift's friend Selena Gomez. Joining Gomez for appearances in the video were more of Swift's friends, including actresses Hailee Steinfeld and Lena Dunham, as well as model Gigi Hadid. In addition, Mariska Hargitay from *Law and Order: Special Victims Unit* and Ellen Pompeo from *Grey's Anatomy* also appeared in the video. Serious Swift fans understood why those two actresses were included. Swift is a fan of the television shows they are on, and her cats are named after the characters they play: Olivia Benson and Meredith Grey, respectively.

1. Quoted in Josh Eells, "The Reinvention of Taylor Swift," *Rolling Stone*, September 8, 2014. www.rollingstone.com/music/features/taylor-swift-1989-cover-story-20140908.

Groundbreaking Grammy Winner

Although "Shake It Off" was nominated for three Grammy Awards in 2015, the rest of *1989* had to wait until 2016 to be nominated for these awards. That year, Swift was nominated for a total of seven Grammy Awards, tying her with The Weeknd for the second highest number of nominations that year—four behind the eleven nominations secured by Kendrick Lamar.

At the Grammy Awards ceremony on February 15, 2016, Swift won three awards for *1989*. "Bad Blood" won for Best Music Video, and the album itself won for Best Pop Vocal Album and Album of the Year. With her Grammy for Album of the Year, Swift became the first woman to win that award twice. In her acceptance speech for the award, she made a pointed statement encouraging women to take ownership of their success, which many believed to be a direct response to Kanye West's claim in his music that he made her famous:

> *As the first woman to win Album of the Year at the Grammys twice, I want to say to all the young women out there: There are going to be people along the way who will try to undercut your success or take credit for your accomplishments or your fame, but if you just focus on the work and you don't let those people sidetrack you, someday when you get where you're going, you'll look around and you'll know that it was you and the people who love you who put you there and that will be the greatest feeling in the world.*[56]

Swift had every reason to believe that she was experiencing "the greatest feeling in the world." She followed her gut and made the kind of album she wanted to make, and it resulted in one of the most coveted awards in the music business.

Swift also opened the 2016 Grammy Awards with a performance of "Out of the Woods."

Max Martin

When Swift won her Grammy Award for Album of the Year in 2016, she took time to single out Max Martin for his work as co-songwriter and producer on the album. Martin—a Swedish songwriter and music producer—was instrumental in Swift's transformation from country singer to pop star, and he began working with her on *Red*'s pop-influenced songs, including "We Are Never Ever Getting Back Together." That was his first number 1 hit on the Hot 100 with Swift. He also earned a nomination alongside Swift for Album of the Year for *Red*.

However, that song was not Martin's first Hot 100 chart-topper. As of late 2015, his songs had topped the Hot 100 chart 21 times, which includes four songs he wrote with Swift. In addition to "We Are Never Ever Getting Back Together," Martin co-wrote the *1989* hits "Shake It Off," "Blank Space," and "Bad Blood."

Martin is best known for his work with female pop singers such as Swift. His first number 1 song on the Hot 100 came in 1999 with Britney Spears's "...Baby One More Time." After that, he wrote and produced hit songs for other female artists, including Pink, Kelly Clarkson, and Katy Perry. Martin also wrote and produced hits for some of the most famous "boy bands" of

On Top of the World

It was no secret that *1989* was a huge financial success. In fact, Swift was named the highest-paid musician in 2015 by *Billboard* magazine, thanks to a combination of album sales, publishing royalties, streaming rights, and touring. The majority of that rev-

the late 1990s and early 2000s, including Backstreet Boys and 'NSYNC.

Before *1989*'s win for Album of the Year, Martin had already been nominated for that award three times. In addition to *Red*, he was nominated for *Millennium* by Backstreet Boys and *Teenage Dream* by Katy Perry.

Max Martin's real name is Karl Martin Sandberg. He is shown here with members of Backstreet Boys.

enue came from her *1989* World Tour. Swift announced the tour in November 2014, and it kicked off in Japan in May 2015. She traveled to Asia, Europe, and Australia, in addition to major cities in the United States and Canada. Swift played in large arenas and stadiums, drawing thousands of fans to her shows each night. The tour brought in $61.7 million, which earned Swift the 2016

Swift's successful world tour helped her earn almost twice as much as the next person on *Billboard*'s list of 2015's highest paid musicians.

Billboard Music Award for Top Touring Artist.

The accolades continued to roll in for Swift after the release of *1989* and its successful tour. Swift was included on *Forbes* magazine's 2015 list of the World's Most Powerful Women, and she made another appearance on *TIME's* 100 Most Influential People list that same year. In 2016, Swift topped *Forbes's* list of the World's Highest-Paid Celebrities. According the magazine, Swift earned $170 million from her music, her tours, and her endorsement deals with various companies. By 2016, Swift had reached new heights as an artist, a businesswoman, and a pop culture phenomenon. In 10 years, she had grown from a teenage girl hoping to have a hit album to an international superstar with five hit albums and passionate fans around the world.

Chapter Five

Beyond the Music

Taylor Swift became famous for her music, but now that is far from the only thing about her that makes headlines. She can be seen in advertisements for major companies, and pictures of her wearing the latest fashion trends can be found in magazines around the world. She has even made appearances in movies and on television shows. Swift is one of the most recognized women in the world, and everything about her—from the clothes she wears to her famous friendships—is dissected by superfans and skeptics alike. Although music is still at the center of Swift's life and her career, there is much to learn about who she is beyond what she reveals in her songs.

Product Partnerships

Swift first appeared in ads for Abercrombie & Fitch as a teenager, but that was just the beginning of her work in advertising campaigns. As Swift's star rose, so did the demand for her to appear in print ads, commercials, and other projects for major brands. In 2009, American Greetings launched a line of greeting cards that used Swift's writing. That same year, she appeared in ads

Taylor Swift is more than just a popular singer. She is also a smart and successful businesswoman.

for the clothing label l.e.i., and she developed her own line of sundresses for that label. Swift has also created her own line of shoes for Keds and has modeled in their advertising campaigns.

In addition to clothing, Swift has appeared in ads for Cover Girl cosmetics and Sony Electronics. In 2013, she was named a brand ambassador for Diet Coke. This partnership involved print, television, and digital ads, as well as exclusive content for Swift's fans provided through Diet Coke's social media pages. In 2014, a Diet Coke ad offered viewers a snippet of one of the songs from

Swift and Apple: Not Always a Partnership

Although Swift became the face of Apple Music in 2016, she was not always on good terms with the music streaming service. In June 2015, she wrote an open letter to Apple on her official Tumblr page, explaining why she would not give the company the ability to stream *1989* on Apple Music, which was still in the development phase at that point. Swift had already taken her music off the streaming service Spotify, writing in the *Wall Street Journal*, "It's my opinion that music should not be free, and my prediction is that individual artists and labels will someday decide what an album's price point is. I hope they don't underestimate themselves or undervalue their art."[1] Swift believed artists should be well compensated for their music being available on streaming services. This was why she was so disappointed in Apple Music, which initially was not going to pay artists for the use of their music during the service's

1989—"How You Get the Girl"—before the album was released. Swift has been described as a "longtime Diet Coke fan,"[57] so the partnership seemed like a natural fit.

One of Swift's most famous advertising partnerships is the one she developed with Apple Music in 2016. In the first of her ads for the music streaming service, she was shown on a treadmill, rapping enthusiastically along with "Jumpman" by Drake and Future until she falls off. The ad went viral, causing a huge spike in downloads for the song. Other Apple Music ads featuring Swift

free three-month trial period.

Swift wrote in her Tumblr post that she was speaking for more artists than just herself:

> *These are not the complaints of a spoiled, petulant child. These are the echoed sentiments of every artist, writer and producer in my social circles who are afraid to speak up because we admire and respect Apple so much.*[2]

Swift knew she would face criticism for pulling her music from streaming services, but she believed she was doing the right thing for herself and for others in the music industry, especially other artists who were not as wealthy or famous as she is. She used her popularity and her power to affect change. Apple later announced that it was going to pay artists whose music was streaming on Apple Music during the free trial period.

1. Taylor Swift, "For Taylor Swift, the Future of Music Is a Love Story," *Wall Street Journal*, July 7, 2014. www.wsj.com/articles/for-taylor-swift-the-future-of-music-is-a-love-story-1404763219.

2. Taylor Swift, "To Apple, Love Taylor," Tumblr, June 21, 2015. taylorswift.tumblr.com/post/122071902085/to-apple-love-taylor.

included her singing along to Jimmy Eat World's "The Middle" before going out and dancing to The Darkness's "I Believe in a Thing Called Love."

Swift also has her own line of perfume that is sold on her official website and through retailers such as Ulta. Swift described the story behind her first two fragrances—Wonderstruck and Wonderstruck Enchanted—as being "about fairytales."[58] Swift's third fragrance made its way into stores in 2013. Taylor by Taylor Swift got its name because, as Swift said when it was announced, "This fragrance is more about my own style, so I wanted the name to be more personal."[59] The perfume was created as a way for the singer's fans to add some of her style into their own lives.

Another way for Swift's fans to copy her style was announced in late 2015. An official Taylor Swift clothing line became available on online platforms such as Tmall and JD.com. In January 2016, Swift's clothing line officially debuted during Hong Kong Fashion Week. The clothing line is made up of shirts, pants, and dresses inspired by Swift's signature style, often featuring the names of her songs, her name, or her initials.

Swift Style

Swift's transition into the world of perfume and clothing made perfect sense considering her status as a contemporary style icon. Her look has changed throughout her career as she has grown as an artist and as a young woman. In a 2016 interview with *Vogue* magazine, Swift said, "Going through different phases is one of my favorite things about fashion. I love how it can mark the passage of time. It's similar to my songs in that way—it all helps identify where I was at different points in my life."[60]

At the beginning of her career, Swift dressed the part of the country music princess, wearing sundresses, cowboy boots, and long, blonde curls. As she started attending more award shows, sequined gowns and shorter dresses became her red carpet trademark. As Swift grew up, so did her outfits. By 2013, she became known for dressing in a way *People* magazine called "retro with a modern flair."[61] Photographs of Swift on the beach showed her wearing high-waisted, two-piece bathing suits, which inspired a major fashion trend. Red lipstick and pearls were also important parts of her look at this time in her life.

Once Swift moved to New York City, photographers began capturing more photos of her on the city streets, and her day-to-day style became even more visible. Around this time, Swift became famous for pairing high-waisted skirts, pants, and shorts with crop tops. Even Swift's gym clothes were shown in fashion magazines and talked about on fashion websites.

Swift's hair has also been a major topic of discussion throughout her career. It was big news when she cut it before the release of *1989*, and it was also big news

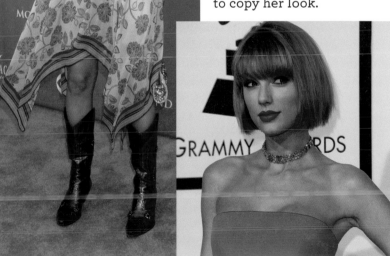

Swift's changing style has inspired many fashion trends as her fans have tried to copy her look.

when she dyed it platinum blonde in April 2016. At that time, Swift's new hair color went along with a more dramatic overall style, with darker lipstick, higher boots, and clothing with a harder edge to it than she'd worn before. Only a few months later, however, Swift was back to a more familiar style. By summer 2016, she was appearing in crop tops, bright red lipstick, and flat shoes again. Swift also dyed her hair back to a darker shade of blonde.

For the majority of her career, Swift's style has fallen into a category *Vogue* reporter Jason Gay called "effortless appropriateness."[62] That label appears to extend to nearly every aspect of her life. Her social media accounts document her adventures baking cakes and cookies, having coffee in her house with friends, and playing with her cats. Although some might agree with *Forbes's* Dani Di Placido, who called her public persona "sickly-sweet,"[63] Swift's fans believe her public image provides young people—especially young women—with a positive role model.

On the Big Screen

Television commercials and fashion magazines aren't the only places where Swift's fans can see her when she is not performing. She has also been featured in movies and on popular television shows. Swift began performing in musical theater productions when she was a child in Wyomissing, and acting has always been something she has enjoyed. In 2012, Swift told MTV News, "Acting is something I've been fascinated by my entire life."[64] Once her music career began to take off, she began to look for the right acting projects.

In 2009, Swift hosted *Saturday Night Live*. She appeared in nearly every skit the night she hosted, and she wrote the song she performed for her monologue. That same year, she appeared in an episode of one of her favorite television shows, *CSI: Crime Scene Investigation*. Many critics praised Swift's work hosting *Saturday Night Live*, but they were less enthusiastic about her work in the crime genre.

Swift, shown here on the red carpet for the film *The Lorax*, has been interested in acting since she was a little girl.

At the time, it seemed comedic roles would play more to Swift's strengths. In 2010, she joined the large ensemble cast of *Valentine's Day*, which starred famous actors such as Julia Roberts, Jennifer Garner, Bradley Cooper, and Taylor Lautner. The film itself did not get rave reviews from many critics, but Swift's fans were determined to show their support for her small part in it. She won the Teen Choice Award for Choice Movie Breakout: Female thanks to their votes.

Two years later, Swift added her voice to the animated adaptation of Dr. Seuss's *The Lorax*. Swift voiced the character of Audrey, and her work earned her another Teen Choice Award—this time for Choice Movie Voice. The next year, Swift appeared in one episode of the television show *New Girl* as the title character in "Elaine's Big Day."

In 2014, Swift returned to the big screen in the film version of Lois Lowry's popular book *The Giver*. Her character, Rosemary, was only mentioned by other characters in the book, but she appeared as a visible memory in the movie. The film itself did not win over critics, and it also did not do well at the box office. However, it did give Swift her first taste of dramatic acting in a major motion picture.

Dating and Double Standards

When Swift appeared in *Valentine's Day*, much of the talk surrounding her role was not about her acting, but instead about the fact that she acted opposite Lautner, whom she was reportedly dating at the time. Swift is no stranger to people focusing more on her relationships than on her work. Her personal approach to songwriting has always invited speculation about which songs were about which famous ex-boyfriend: Lautner, Joe Jonas, John Mayer, Jake Gyllenhaal, Harry Styles, or someone else. Although Swift has found success channeling her private life into her music, she has said that a line needs to be drawn between fans seeing her life reflected in her songs and her dating life becoming national news. She told *Rolling Stone*, "I don't like it when headlines read

'Careful, Bro, She'll Write a Song About You,' because it trivializes my work."[65] Swift has worked hard to prove that she is more than just a girl who got famous by singing songs about famous men. However, the public scrutiny of her love life has only increased as her star has risen.

That intense scrutiny caused Swift to shy away from dating anyone for a period of time. She had grown tired of being publicly criticized for dating different people, which she saw as evidence of a double standard that shamed her for dating and writing songs about her experiences in a way that she felt does not happen with male singer-songwriters. In an interview with *Vogue*, Swift said, "I went out on a normal amount of dates in my early 20s, and I got absolutely slaughtered for it … I didn't date for two and a half years. Should I have had to do that? No."[66] Swift has spent much of her career trying to find a balance between being open enough in her songs to honestly connect with her fans and still maintaining a healthy amount of privacy when it comes to her love life. That is not an easy balance to achieve.

"It's Not a Tragedy"

Swift went a long time without dating anyone around the time *1989* was released. Although she felt she should not have had to stop dating because of public scrutiny, she did learn a lot from her time without a boyfriend. In 2014, she told *Esquire* magazine,

> I think it's healthy for everyone to go a few years without dating, just because you need to get to know who you are. And I've done more thinking and examining and figuring out how to cope with things on my own than I would have if I had been focusing on someone else's emotions and someone else's schedule.[67]

Swift's time on her own inspired some of the songs on *1989*, and she discovered that she did not need to be in a relationship to be happy—contrary to what anyone else might think. Swift told *Rolling Stone*, "It's not bad that I'm not hopelessly in love with someone. It's not a tragedy, and it's not me giving up and being a spinster."[68] By taking some time to be single, Swift showed her young fans that they do not need to be in a relationship in order to be happy. In her *Esquire* interview, Swift added, "I do not need some guy around in order to get inspiration, in order to make a great record, in order to live my life, in order to feel okay about myself. And I wanted to show my fans the same thing."[69] Swift had her work, family, and friends, and for a time, that was all she needed to feel fulfilled.

Dating Drama

In March 2015, Swift began dating Scottish musician and songwriter Calvin Harris, whose real name is Adam Richard Wiles. Swift and Harris's relationship was documented in the press and through social media, and it was the most public Swift had ever been about a romantic relationship to that point. However, the relationship ended in June 2016, and both parties deleted almost all the evidence of their relationship from their social media accounts.

What seemed to be an amicable split turned ugly after news broke that Swift had written Harris's hit song "This Is What You Came For" under the pseudonym, or pen name, Nils Sjöberg. Harris then went on Twitter to share his displeasure that Swift allowed the news to come out the way it did about a song he claimed he still worked hard to create. According to the *Washington Post*, Harris wrote on Twitter, "I wrote the music, produced the song, arranged it and cut the vocals … Hurtful to me at this point that her and her team would go so far out of their way to try to make ME look bad at this stage though."[70]

Some of the tension between Harris and Swift seemed to stem from Swift's new relationship with popular actor Tom Hiddleston, whom she began dating not long after her breakup with Harris was made public. Swift and Hiddleston were photographed together in Rhode Island, Italy, and Australia in just the first few

Swift referred to Harris, shown with her here, as her boyfriend in an acceptance speech at the iHeartRadio Music Awards in April 2016. This was a first for Swift, who had previously been incredibly guarded when it came to revealing specific details about her private life in any situation.

months of their relationship. The speed at which their relationship developed led some to claim that the romance was fake. Pop culture writer Libby Hill summed up the speculation surrounding their relationship in a piece in the *Los Angeles Times*, in which she wrote, "The couple's rapidly intensifying relationship gives off a stench of something false."[71] Some claimed the relationship is a piece of performance art; others believed it was a publicity stunt to keep their names in the headlines and possibly further their careers.

Despite the elaborate conspiracy theories surrounding them, Swift and Hiddleston continued to be open about their relationship. In a July 2016 interview with the *Hollywood Reporter*, Hiddleston said, "The truth is that Taylor Swift and I are together, and we're very happy … That's the truth. It's not a publicity stunt."[72] However, that did not remain the truth for long. In early September 2016, the two announced that their relationship was over.

Dating in the public eye is nothing new to Swift, but its challenges have not gone away with time. Swift once called the fascination with her dating life "a national pastime,"[73] and that fascination shows no signs of going away as long as Swift continues to be in the spotlight.

Swift's Squad

If Swift had her way, she would be known for a different kind of relationship than the ones that typically dominate the headlines when it comes to her life. Friendship has become increasingly important to Swift, especially since the period of time she spent away from the dating scene prior to *1989*'s release. In her 2014 interview with *Rolling Stone*, she described why being single helped her build a strong support system of female friends:

When your number-one priority is getting a boyfriend, you're more inclined to see a beautiful girl and think, 'Oh, she's gonna get that hot guy I wish I was dating.' But when you're not boy-friend-shopping, you're able to step back and see other girls who are killing it and think, 'God, I want to be around her.'[74]

Swift's group of friends has become known as her "squad," and the women who are included in it are some of the most power-

Swift was once known only for her romantic relationships, but she is now also known for her friendships with other famous women.

A Feminist Point of View

Swift now proudly calls herself a feminist, but she was not always quick to embrace that title. In a 2014 interview with the *Guardian* newspaper, Swift said, "As a teenager, I didn't understand that saying you're a feminist is just saying that you hope women and men will have equal rights and equal opportunities ... For so long, it's been made to seem like something where you'd picket against the opposite sex, whereas it's not about that at all."[1] Becoming friends with outspoken feminist Lena Dunham helped Swift embrace that part of herself. As Dunham told *Rolling Stone*, "She runs her own company, she's creating music that connects to other women ... and no one is in control of her. If that's not feminism, what is?"[2] Swift and her friends also consider their "squad" to be a strong example of the feminist idea of women supporting other women.

However, not everyone believes Swift has a firm grasp of the concept of feminism. In a 2015 *Washington Post* article, Jill Filipovic wrote, "Feminism is more than just

ful young women in their respective fields. However, Swift has not left behind the friends she made before becoming a superstar, including Abigail Anderson and Britany LaManna. Swift was even the maid of honor at LaManna's 2016 wedding to another one of her childhood friends, Benjamin LaManna. She remains close to both LaManna and Anderson, inviting them to her star-studded parties alongside the more famous members of her group of friends.

One of Swift's oldest friends in the entertainment industry is

supporting your girlfriends or churning out charming catchphrases about girl power; it's a political movement … Certainly, the feminism of someone like Swift is genuine, but that doesn't mean it runs particularly deep."[3] Filipovic and other critics have claimed that Swift's brand of feminism is directed only toward supporting her friends and celebrating her own accomplishments, without enough focus on women outside of her own friends and fans, especially women of color. No matter what people might think of Swift's interpretation of feminism, it is clear that she has helped open many people's eyes—especially many young women's eyes—to the conversations and debates surrounding the modern understanding of what it means to be a feminist.

1. Quoted in Hermione Hoby, "Taylor Swift: 'Sexy? Not on My Radar,'" *Guardian*, August 23, 2014. www.theguardian.com/music/2014/aug/23/taylor-swift-shake-it-off.

2. Quoted in Josh Eells, "The Reinvention of Taylor Swift," *Rolling Stone*, September 8, 2014. www.rollingstone.com/music/features/taylor-swift-1989-cover-story-20140908.

3. Jill Filipovic, "Sorry, Taylor Swift. Being a Feminist Is About More Than Just Supporting Your Girlfriends," *Washington Post*, July 23, 2015. www.washingtonpost.com/posteverything/wp/2015/07/23/sorry-taylor-swift-being-a-feminist-is-about-more-than-just-supporting-your-girlfriends/?utm_term=.abd6da64c350.

Selena Gomez, who rose to fame as a singer and an actress. Swift has become good friends with many models, too, including Gigi Hadid, Martha Hunt, and Cara Delevingne, who also starred in the movie *Paper Towns*. One of Swift's best friends is the famous model Karlie Kloss. Their friendship has taken center stage at fashion shows and on the cover of *Vogue* in 2015. In that cover story, Kloss said, "You know, real friends are hard to find—and Taylor's a real friend. There's nothing better."[75] Gomez, Hadid, Hunt, Delevingne, and Kloss all appeared in Swift's "Bad Blood" music video. They also all appeared alongside Swift and some of the other women from the music video on the red carpet at the 2015 MTV VMAs.

Swift's group of friends also includes a number of talented musicians, including the Haim sisters: Alana, Danielle, and Este. Ed Sheeran is another close friend of Swift's, and the two collaborated on the song "Everything Has Changed," which was featured on *Red*. In addition, Swift became close friends with Lena Dunham, who wrote and starred in one of Swift's favorite television shows, *Girls*. Dunham has spoken highly of Swift, telling *Vogue*, "If something good happens to me … I get a text from Taylor way before I get a text from my mom."[76] Their friendship inspired Swift to become more outspoken about feminist issues.

After spending much of her time in Wyomissing feeling like an outcast, Swift has devoted herself to amassing a large group of friends. Although some have stated that this "squad" is "exclusive"[77] and similar to the groups of girls who once excluded Swift in school, her friends argue that what they have formed is something genuinely supportive. Hadid told a reporter for *Elle Canada*:

> We want to be the generation and the group of friends known for supporting each other. "Squad Goals" is a big social-media thing right now, and that's what we want to inspire in other groups of friends—to be proud of the power you all have together, which can be amplified so much by each person.[78]

Swift never felt like the cool girl in school, but she is now at the center of the world's most famous "squad."

Making a Difference

Feminism is one of the causes close to Swift's heart, but it is not the only cause she is passionate about. Swift has been involved in numerous philanthropic efforts throughout her career. In

2007, she joined with Tennessee governor Phil Bredesen and the Tennessee Association of Chiefs of Police to start an initiative called Delete Online Predators. The goal of this initiative was to educate young people and their parents about Internet safety and to combat Internet sex crimes.

Swift's charitable endeavors did not stop there. The next year, she donated $100,000 to the American Red Cross to help people affected by a devastating flood in Cedar Rapids, Iowa. Swift also gives large amounts of money to schools. In 2015, it was announced that she had donated $50,000 from the sales of the song "Welcome to New York" to the New York City Department of Education.

Swift's generosity and outspoken support of causes that matter to her helped secure her a spot at the top of the "Celebs Gone Good" list compiled by the advocacy website DoSomething.org. This list is meant to highlight celebrities who do positive things with their money and fame. Swift topped the list three years in a row—from 2012 to 2014. She has supported many other charitable and philanthropic organizations, including Habitat for Humanity, UNICEF, Feeding America, and Stand Up to Cancer.

In August 2016, deadly and destructive floods overtook parts of Louisiana. When Swift heard about the disaster, she wanted to help. She pledged to donate $1 million to help those affected by the floods. In an official statement, Swift said, "We began The *1989* World Tour in Louisiana, and the wonderful fans there made us feel completely at home. The fact that so many people in Louisiana have been forced out of their own homes this week is heartbreaking."[79] By making a donation that made headlines around the country, Swift also raised awareness for this important cause.

Giving Back to Her Fans

Just like her music, giving back is something that is very personal for Swift. As such, she has been known to reach out to her fans individually in both big and small ways. Swift sometimes comments on Tumblr or Instagram posts written by fans who are going through hard times, offering support and encouragement. She has also sent surprise packages to fans, including Ally Moronese. In 2015, Swift saw a post Moronese made on Tumblr in which she shared that she was having a hard time dealing with moving out of her childhood home. Swift then sent Moronese a care package that included a blanket, a pillow, candles, a notebook, and a handwritten note. Swift wrote, "I check in on you all the time because you're smart and hysterically funny and beautiful. You deserve to be happy and I just hope these presents make you smile."[80] Establishing such a strong personal connection with her fans is one of the reasons why Swift has such a passionate following.

Swift wanted to celebrate her fans in a big way around Christmas 2014. That year, she selected a group of them and took time to learn about them through their social media accounts. She then mailed them boxes of Christmas gifts tailored to their interests, as well as personal cards she wrote to them. Her fans dubbed the event "Swiftmas," and a video showing Swift wrapping the gifts and her fans excitedly opening them became extremely popular online. The fans who received the gifts were genuinely touched by the gesture. Rebecca Cox was 16 years old when she received her "Swiftmas" gifts, and she told *Billboard*, "There's no one in the music industry who has as big of a heart as [Swift] does."[81]

Swift has surprised her fans with appearances at major events in their lives. She visited a fan's bridal shower in 2014 and gave her gifts for her kitchen. In 2016, she surprised a couple at their wedding and performed during their reception. Swift also spends time with fans who are sick, visiting them in the hospital or taking them out to eat and talking with them. Her dedication to showing her fans—who sometimes call themselves "Swifties"—that she cares about them on a personal level is a huge part of Swift's success.

A Wide-Open Future

Taylor Swift has been in the public eye for more than a decade. Along the way, she has often shown herself to be a hard worker and a detailed planner. However, when asked in early 2016 about her plans for the next stages of her life and career, she answered, "I have no idea. This is the first time in ten years that I haven't known ... I decided I was going to live my life a little bit without the pressure on myself to create something."[82] Although Swift has stated that she has no intention of giving up the music that has made her a household name around the world, she was not pushing herself to write new songs after the release of *1989*. However, because her style of songwriting is inspired so famously by her life, it is clear that she will be compiling material for new music, even if she has no plans to record that music in the immediate future.

No matter where Swift's career choices and personal relationships may take her in the future, she will always be known as one of the most famous songwriters of her generation. She has given her fans a voice, and in return, they have helped her rise to the top of the music industry.

Notes

Introduction: Making It Personal

1. Jon Caramanica, "Sounds of Swagger and Sob Stories," *New York Times*, December 19, 2008. www.nytimes.com/2008/12/21/arts/music/21cara.html?_r=2.

2. Quoted in James Hibberd, "Swift Talks Favorite Christmas Songs, Next Album," *Entertainment Weekly*, December 23, 2013. www.ew.com/article/2013/12/23/taylor-swift-christmas.

3. Quoted in J. Freedom du Lac, "Her Song: Talking Taylor Swift," *Washington Post*, February 28, 2008. voices.washingtonpost.com/postrock/2008/02/her_song_talking_taylor_swift_1.html.

4. Randy Lewis, "Taylor Swift Doesn't Just Use Social Media for Crafty Marketing—She's Making True Fan Connections," *Los Angeles Times*, August 27, 2015. www.latimes.com/entertainment/music/posts/la-et-ms-taylor-swift-1989-tour-staples-social-media-20150827-htmlstory.html.

5. Lewis, "Making True Fan Connections."

6. Emily Yahr, "Taylor Swift Just Can't Help Herself," *Washington Post*, July 11, 2016. www.washingtonpost.com/news/arts-and-entertainment/wp/2016/07/11/taylor-swift-just-cant-help-herself/.

7. Lewis, "Making True Fan Connections."

8. Quoted in Associated Press, "Taylor Swift Is Living Out Her Childhood Dream," MSNBC.com, May 27, 2009. today.msnbc.msn.com/id/30968285/ns/today-entertainment.

Chapter One: Pennsylvania Roots

9. Quoted in Jocelyn Vena, "Taylor Swift Explains Why 13 Is Her Lucky Number," MTV.com, May 7, 2009. www.mtv.com/news/1610839/taylor-swift-explains-why-13-is-her-lucky-number/.

10. Quoted in Richard Rhys, "Exit Interview: Taylor Swift," *Philadelphia*, October 21, 2008. www.phillymag.com/articles/exit-interview-taylor-swift/.

11. Quoted in du Lac, "Her Song."

12. Quoted in du Lac, "Her Song."

13. Quoted in Katie Couric's "All Access" Grammy Special, CBS, January

9, 2009. www.cbsnews.com/video/watch/?id=4763359n.

14. Quoted in du Lac, "Her Song."

15. Quoted in Edward Morris, "When She Thinks 'Tim McGraw,' Taylor Swift Savors Payoff," CMT.com, December 1, 2006. www.cmt.com/news/country-music/1546980/when-she-thinks-tim-mcgraw-taylor-swift-savors-payoff.jhtml.

16. Quoted in CMT.com, "20 Questions with Taylor Swift," November 12, 2007. www.cmt.com/news/1574118/20-questions-with-taylor-swift/.

17. Quoted in Daphne Merkin, "The Story Teller," *Allure*, April 2009, p. 192.

18. Quoted in Lauren Waterman, "Swift Ascent," *Teen Vogue*, March 2009, p. 135.

19. Quoted in Bruce DeMara, "Taylor Swift: Country Music's Rising Star," *Toronto Star*, December 1, 2008. www.thestar.com/entertainment/article/292927.

20. Quoted in Edd Hurt, "Taylor Swift: Elevating Teen Dreams into Art," *American Songwriter*, December 12, 2008. www.americansongwriter.com/2008/12/taylor-swift-elevating-teen-dreams-into-art.

21. Quoted in Rory Evans, "Interview with Taylor Swift: She's Living Her Taylor-Made Dream," *Women's Health*, December 2008. www.womenshealthmag.com/life/taylor-swift-interview.

Chapter Two: Dreams Come True in Nashville

22. Taylor Swift, "The 10 Women who Changed My Life," *Glamour UK*, May 1, 2015. www.glamourmagazine.co.uk/celebrity/celebrity-galleries/2015/05/taylor-swift-the-10-women-who-changed-my-life/viewgallery/1395866.

23. Quoted in Chris Willman, "Getting to Know Taylor Swift," *Entertainment Weekly*, July 25, 2007. www.ew.com/article/2007/07/25/getting-know-taylor-swift.

24. Quoted in Hurt, "Taylor Swift."

25. Quoted in Dale Kawashima, "Special Interview (2007): Taylor Swift Discusses Her Debut Album, Early Hits, and How She Got Started," Songwriter Universe, February 16, 2007. www.songwriteruniverse.com/taylorswift123.htm.

26. Quoted in Vanessa Grigoriadis, "The Very Pink, Very Perfect Life of Taylor Swift," *Rolling Stone*, March 5, 2009.

www.rollingstone.com/music/news/the-very-pink-very-perfect-life-of-taylor-swift-20090305.

27. Quoted in Joe Edwards, Associated Press, "For Teen Country Star Taylor Swift, the Time Was Just Right," *Seattle Times*, January 26, 2007. www.seattletimes.com/entertainment/for-teen-country-star-taylor-swift-the-time-was-just-right/.

28. Quoted in Kawashima, "Special Interview (2007)."

29. Quoted in Edward Morris, "Taylor Swift Emerges as Country's Golden Girl," CTM.com, February 23, 2007. www.cmt.com/news/country-music/1553127/taylor-swift-emerges-as-countrys-golden-girl.jhtml.

Chapter Three: Superstar Status

30. Quoted in Morris, "When She Thinks 'Tim McGraw.'"

31. Jody Rosen, "Taylor Swift: Fearless," *Rolling Stone*, November 13, 2008. www.rollingstone.com/music/albumreviews/fearless-20081113.

32. Quoted in Austin Scaggs, "Taylor's Time: Catching Up with Taylor Swift," *Rolling Stone*, January 25, 2010. www.rollingstone.com/music/news/taylors-time-catching-up-with-taylor-swift-20100125.

33. Quoted in Hoda Kotb, "On Tour with Taylor Swift," *Dateline NBC* transcript, May 31, 2009. www.nbcnews.com/id/31032270/ns/dateline_nbc-newsmakers/t/tour-taylor-swift/#.V6jqYpMrKjh.

34. Chris Willman, "Album Review: Taylor Swift's 'Speak Now,'" *Hollywood Reporter*, October 19, 2010. www.hollywoodreporter.com/review/taylor-swift-speak-album-31396.

35. Elysa Gardner, "When Taylor Swift Speaks on New Album, You Should Listen," *USA Today*, October 21, 2010. www.usatoday.com/life/music/reviews/2010-10-22-taylorswift22_VA_N.htm.

36. Emily Yahr, "Of Course Taylor Swift Should Write Songs About Calvin Harris. It's Literally Her Job.," *Washington Post*, June 3, 2016. www.washingtonpost.com/news/arts-and-entertainment/wp/2016/06/03/of-course-taylor-swift-should-write-songs-about-calvin-harris-its-literally-her-job/.

37. Quoted in Academy of Country Music Awards, CBS, April 3, 2011.

38. "Taylor Swift, 'Red': Track-By-Track Review," *Billboard*, October 19, 2012. www.billboard.com/articles/review/1066798/taylor-swift-red-track-by-track-review.

39. Jon Caramanica, "No More Kid Stuff for Taylor Swift," *New York*

Times, October 24, 2012. www.nytimes.com/2012/10/28/arts/music/no-more-kid-stuff-for-taylor-swift.html?_r=0.

40. "Taylor Swift, 'Red': Track-By-Track Review."

Chapter Four: The Next Chapter

41. Taylor Swift, "The Songs Were Once About My Life. They Are Now About Yours." TaylorSwift.com, October 27, 2014. taylorswift.com/about_from_taylor.

42. Swift, "They Are Now About Yours."

43. Quoted in Rob Sheffield, "The Taylor Swift Guide to 1989: Breakers Gonna Break, Fakers Gonna Fake," *Rolling Stone*, September 8, 2014. www.rollingstone.com/music/lists/taylor-swift-guide-to-1989-20140908.

44. Josh Eells, "The Reinvention of Taylor Swift," *Rolling Stone*, September 8, 2014. www.rollingstone.com/music/features/taylor-swift-1989-cover-story-20140908.

45. Quoted in Randy Lewis, "How Does Taylor Swift Connect with Fans? 'Secret Sessions' and Media Blitzes," *Los Angeles Times*, October 28, 2014. www.latimes.com/entertainment/music/la-et-ms-taylor-swift-1989-secret-sessions-fans-20141028-story.html.

46. Quoted in Lewis, "'Secret Sessions' and Media Blitzes."

47. Quoted in Alan Light, "Billboard Woman of the Year Taylor Swift on Writing Her Own Rules, Not Becoming a Cliché and the Hurdle of Going Pop," *Billboard*, December 5, 2014. www.billboard.com/articles/events/women-in-music-2014/6363514/billboard-woman-of-the-year-taylor-swift-on-writing-her.

48. Swift, "They Are Now About Yours."

49. Quoted in Eells, "Reinvention of Taylor Swift."

50. Jon Caramanica, "A Farewell to Twang," *New York Times*, October 23, 2014. www.nytimes.com/2014/10/26/arts/music/taylor-swift-1989-new-album-review.html?_r=0.

51. Mikael Wood, "Taylor Swift Smooths Out the Wrinkles on Sleek '1989,'" *Los Angeles Times*, October 27, 2014. www.latimes.com/entertainment/music/la-et-ms-review-taylor-swift-smooths-out-the-wrinkles-on-sleek-1989-20141027-story.html.

52. Caramanica, "A Farwell to Twang."

53. Caramanica, "A Farewell to Twang."

54. Wood, "Taylor Swift Smooths Out the Wrinkles."

55. Quoted in Eells, "Reinvention of Taylor Swift."

56. Quoted in Grammy Awards, CBS, February 15, 2016.

Chapter Five: Beyond the Music

57. "Taylor Swift Gets a Taste of Her Favorite Things in New Diet Coke Commercial," The Coca-Cola Company, October 15, 2014. www.coca-colacompany.com/stories/taylor-swift-gets-a-taste-of-her-favorite-things-in-new-diet-coke-commercial.

58. Quoted in Alex Apatoff, "Exclusive First Look: Taylor Swift's Newest Perfume," *People*, May 29, 2013. site.people.com/style/exclusive-first-look-taylor-swifts-newest-perfume/.

59. Quoted in Apatoff, "Taylor Swift's Newest Perfume."

60. Quoted in Jason Gay, "Taylor Swift as You've Never Seen Her Before," *Vogue*, April 14, 2016. www.vogue.com/13421986/taylor-swift-may-cover-maid-of-honor-dating-personal-style/.

61. Apatoff, "Taylor Swift's Newest Perfume."

62. Gay, "Taylor Swift as You've Never Seen Her Before."

63. Dani Di Placido, "Taylor Swift's Carefully Cultivated Image Is Starting to Crack," *Forbes*, July 18, 2016. www.forbes.com/sites/danidiplacido/2016/07/18/taylor-swifts-carefully-cultivated-image-is-starting-to-crack/2/#d0d15565bc35.

64. Quoted in Archive-Azia-Celestino, "Taylor Swift 'Fascinated' by Acting," MTV.com, February 29, 2012. www.mtv.com/news/1680175/taylor-swift-acting-lorax/.

65. Quoted in Eells, "Reinvention of Taylor Swift."

66. Quoted in Gay, "Taylor Swift as You've Never Seen Her Before."

67. Quoted in Scott Raab, "Why Taylor Swift Welcomed You to New York," *Esquire*, October 20, 2014. www.esquire.com/entertainment/music/a30491/taylor-swift-1114/.

68. Quoted in Eells, "Reinvention of Taylor Swift."

69. Quoted in Rabb, "Why Taylor Swift Welcomed You."

70. Quoted in Emily Yahr, "Calvin Harris Broke All the Rules of Taylor Swift's World. Or Did He?," *Washington Post*, July 15, 2016. www.washingtonpost.com/news/arts-and-entertainment/wp/2016/07/15/calvin-harris-broke-all-the-rules-of-taylor-swifts-world-or-did-he/.

71. Libby Hill, "Taylor Swift and Tom Hiddleston: Is Their Relationship an Elaborate Hoax?," *Los Angeles Times*, July 6, 2014.

www.latimes.com/entertainment/gossip/la-et-mg-taylor-swift-tom-hiddleston-20160706-snap-htmlstory.html.

72. Quoted in Bryn Elise Sandberg, "Tom Hiddleston Talks Emmy Nomination, Responds to Taylor Swift Conspiracy Theories (Q&A)," *Hollywood Reporter*, July 14, 2016. www.hollywoodreporter.com/news/tom-hiddleston-talks-emmy-nomination-911178.

73. Quoted in Eells, "Reinvention of Taylor Swift."

74. Quoted in Eells, "Reinvention of Taylor Swift."

75. Quoted in Jada Yuan, "On the Road with Best Friends Taylor Swift and Karlie Kloss," *Vogue*, February 13, 2015. www.vogue.com/9287379/taylor-swift-karlie-kloss-best-friends-march-2015-cover/.

76. Quoted in Yuan, "On the Road."

77. Emilee Lindner, "How Taylor Swift's Squad Divided Our Conversation About Female Friendship," MTV.com, December 31, 2015. www.mtv.com/news/2692497/people-like-to-talk-about-taylor-swifts-girl-squad/.

78. Quoted in Vanessa Craft, "Exclusive: Gigi Hadid on Changing the Modelling Industry, Social Media, and #Squadgoals," *Elle Canada*, September 29, 2015. www.ellecanada.com/culture/celebrity/article/exclusive-gigi-hadid-on-changing-the-modelling-industry-social-media-and-squadgoals.

79. Quoted in Mesfin Fekadu, "AP Exclusive: Taylor Swift Donating $1 Million to Louisiana," *U.S. News & World Report*, August 16, 2016. www.usnews.com/news/entertainment/articles/2016-08-16/ap-exclusive-taylor-swift-donating-1-million-to-louisiana.

80. Quoted in Danielle Tullo, "Taylor Swift Sent a Troubled Fan a Care Package That Will Melt Your Heart," *Cosmopolitan*, July 12, 2015. www.cosmopolitan.com/entertainment/celebs/news/a33327/taylor-swift-now-sending-fans-christmas-care-packages/.

81. Quoted in Jenna Wang, "Fans on Taylor Swift's 'Swiftmas': 'No One in the Industry Has as Big a Heart as She Does," *Billboard*, December 24, 2014. www.billboard.com/articles/columns/pop-shop/6415161/taylor-swift-swiftmas.

82. Quoted in Gay, "Taylor Swift as You've Never Seen Her Before."

Taylor Swift Year by Year

1989

Taylor Swift is born December 13 in Wyomissing, Pennsylvania.

2001

Swift visits Nashville for the first time to begin handing out her demo CD.

2003

Swift gets an artist development deal with RCA Records and is chosen to model in Abercrombie & Fitch's "Rising Star" campaign.

2004

The Swift family moves to Tennessee to help further Taylor's music career; she performs at the Bluebird Café in front of Scott Borchetta.

2005

Borchetta signs Swift to his new label, Big Machine Records.

2006

Swift releases her first single, "Tim McGraw," and releases her debut album, *Taylor Swift*.

2007

Swift tours with Rascal Flatts, George Strait and Ronnie Milsap, Brad Paisley, and Faith Hill and Tim McGraw; serves as the spokesperson for a public education campaign called Delete Online Predators; and releases EP titled *Sounds of the Season: The Taylor Swift Holiday Collection*.

2008

Swift releases *Beautiful Eyes* EP and second album, *Fearless*.

2009

Swift wins four Grammy Awards for *Fearless*; embarks on the *Fearless* tour; hosts *Saturday Night Live*; partners with American Greetings to create a line of greeting cards; and is interrupted by Kanye West during her acceptance speech at the MTV Video Music Awards.

2010

Swift appears in the film *Valentine's Day*; releases third album, *Speak Now*; and is listed on *TIME* magazine's annual list of the 100 most influential people in the world.

2011

Swift kicks off the world tour for *Speak Now* and wins two Grammy Awards.

2012

Swift releases her fourth album, *Red*, and lends her voice to the animated film *The Lorax*.

2013

Swift becomes a brand ambassador for Diet Coke.

2014

Swift moves to New York City; is named a Global Welcome Ambassador for Tourism; appears in the film *The Giver*; and releases her fifth album, *1989*.

2015

The *1989* World Tour begins; Swift writes an open letter to Apple criticizing their lack of compensation for Apple Music artists; *TIME* again names Swift one of the 100 most influential people in the world; Ryan Adams releases a *1989* cover album.

2016

Swift wins three Grammy Awards; is named *Forbes* magazine's highest-paid celebrity in the world; partners with Apple Music; and donates $1 million to flood victims in Louisiana.

For More Information

Books

Burlingame, Jeff. *Taylor Swift: Music Superstar*. Berkeley Heights, NJ: Enslow Publishers, 2012.
This closer look at Taylor Swift provides essential facts about her early life, career, and charity work..

Conroy, Tyler. *Taylor Swift: This Is Our Song*. New York, NY: Simon & Schuster, 2016.
This book contains personal writing, photographs, and artwork submitted by some of Taylor Swift's biggest fans, as well as articles written about Swift's career from the launch of her first album through 2016.

Morreale, Marie. *Taylor Swift*. New York, NY: Children's Press, 2015.
Morreale gives readers an in-depth look at Swift's chart-topping career and the "Swifties" who have grown with her.

Newkey-Burden, Chas. *Taylor Swift Unauthorized: The Whole Story*. London, UK: HarperCollins, 2014.
Newkey-Burden's account of Swift's rise to fame provides essential details about the personal life that has shaped Swift's music.

Spencer, Liv. *Taylor Swift: The Platinum Edition*. Toronto, Canada: ECW Press, 2013.
Spencer's biography presents facts about Swift's life and career through 2013 in great detail.

Websites

The GRAMMYs: Taylor Swift (www.grammy.com/artist/taylor-swift)

The official website of the Grammy Awards lists the awards Swift has won, as well as photos and videos of Swift at Grammy Awards ceremonies throughout her career.

Taylor Swift (taylorswift.com)
Swift's official website provides links to the latest news about her, a forum to connect with other fans, and links to listen to music and buy merchandise.

Taylor Swift: Billboard (www.billboard.com/artist/371422/ taylor-swift)
Billboard magazine's Taylor Swift page features her chart history, articles about her most newsworthy moments, and photos and videos.

Taylor Swift: Born in 1989. (taylorswift.tumblr.com)
Swift's official Tumblr page is filled with photos and personal messages she shares with her followers.

Taylor Swift on Instagram (www.instagram.com/taylorswift)
Swift often uses Instagram to share personal photographs to give her fans a more intimate look at her life.

Taylor Swift on Twitter (twitter.com/taylorswift13)
Swift posts short messages and links to important content using Twitter, which fans can also use to send short messages to her.

Taylor Swift VEVO (www.youtube.com/user/ TaylorSwiftVEVO)
This is the official YouTube page for Swift's music videos and behind-the-scenes video content.

Index

Picture Credits

Cover, p. 65 Helga Esteb/Shutterstock.com; p. 7 Mark Davis/ Getty Images Entertainment/Getty Images; p. 9 Christopher Polk/ ACMA2014/Getty Images Entertainment/Getty Images; p. 14 National News/ZUMA Press; p. 17 Cooper Neill/Getty Images Entertainment/Getty Images; p. 21 Christine Goodwin/TAS/Getty Images Entertainment/Getty Images; p. 24 Christopher Polk/ ACMA2010/Getty Images Entertainment/Getty Images; pp. 29, 63 Kevin Mazur/WireImage/Getty Images; p. 33 B.A.E. Inc./Alamy Stock Photo; pp. 34, 43, 73 (left) Jeff Kravitz/FilmMagic, Inc/ Getty Images; p. 38 Rusty Russell/Getty Images Entertainment/ Getty Images; p. 41 Steve Granitz/WireImage/Getty Images; p. 47 WENN Ltd/Alamy Stock Photo; p. 49 Kevin Kane/Getty Images Entertainment/Getty Images; p. 51 Alo Ceballos/GC Images/ Getty Images; p. 55 Michael Porro/Getty Images Entertainment/ Getty Images; p. 59 Dave Hogan/Hulton Archive/Getty Images; p. 60 Karwai Tang/WireImage/Getty Images; p. 66 Bob Levey/ Getty Images Entertainment/Getty Images; p. 69 Gregg DeGuire/ FilmMagic/Getty Images; p. 73 (right) VALERIE MACON/AFP/ Getty Images; p. 75 Jason Merritt/Getty Images Entertainment/ Getty Images; p. 79 Kevin Mazur/Getty Images Entertainment/ Getty Images; p. 81 Jeff Kravitz/MTV1415/FilmMagic, Inc/ Getty Images.

About the Author

Katie Kawa is the author of numerous books for children and young adults on topics that include history, women's studies, and sports. She graduated from Canisius College in Buffalo, New York, where she majored in both English and Communication Studies. She lives in Western New York with her family and spends her spare time teaching students at a local dance studio and writing about pop culture.